TRAGEDY IN THE
NORTH WOODS

TRAGEDY IN THE
NORTH WOODS

THE
MURDERS OF
JAMES HICKS

TRUDY IRENE SCEE

Charleston   London

THE
History
PRESS

Published by The History Press
Charleston, SC 29403
www.historypress.net

First published 2009

Manufactured in the United States

ISBN 978.1.59629.550.6

Library of Congress CIP data applied for.

We all have our own gifts and abundance, our own sorrows and poverty.
To those who suffered from the violence described herein, or from violence
and loss like this, this book is dedicated.

And to Mary Louise Scee Engleke
My Mother

CONTENTS

ACKNOWLEDGEMENTS

James Rodney Hicks, Maine's serial killer, affected the lives of many people over the course of three decades. He left a trail of destruction behind, as well as decades' worth of police and legal documents. I would like to thank everyone who spoke with me and shared their memories, photographs and documents. In particular, I would like to thank Deputy Attorney General William Stokes; Nancy Hersey; Joseph Zamboni, former Maine State Police detective and now a criminology professor for Maine's Husson College; James Ricker, former Newport police chief and now Newport town manager; Rose Mannette of the Penobscot County Sheriff's Department; Tammy Price; Linda and Wayne Elston; the Brewer Police Department; and a few others who wished to remain nameless. I would also like to express my appreciation to Lance Warren and the staff of The History Press for all of their aid and their forbearance of my lagging technology skills.

In addition, I would like to thank my friends and family who have had to listen to my research and writing woes once again, and this time for an often unpleasant story. In particular, I wish to thank my daughter, Mariah Irene Alainor Ruth Cameron Scee, for her continued fortitude in dealing with a "scribbling" mother.

CHAPTER ONE

HELL BEGINS

A Wife Goes Missing, The Case of Jennie Lynn Cyr Hicks

No one knew where Jennie Lynn Hicks went on that day in July 1977. Perhaps to deliver a birthday cake. Perhaps to visit her sister. No one really knew where Jennie went—they only knew that she did not come home that night, or the next one or the one after that. Five years later, no one knew where Jerilyn Towers went one night after visiting a local bar, and fourteen years after that, no one knew where Lynn Willette went one May evening. All three women had family and friends, people who loved them. None had a compelling enough reason to leave her home and loved ones for good, yet all three did. Whether into the Maine woods or into an urban area, no one knew where the women might have gone. Some people did have their suspicions, however, or—perhaps more aptly put—their fears.

Jennie Lynn Hicks was twenty-three years old in July 1977. She had two young children and a husband a few years older, a husband she had met and married while in high school. Jennie, an attractive young woman with longish, light hair, wore eyeglasses—dark, plastic, angular glasses that she needed quite badly. Her family lived in a trailer park in small-town, mid-state Maine. Jennie worked in a nursing home part time. Her relationship with her parents was sometimes difficult, and the one with her husband was often extremely so. It seems that Jennie's life was not going in the direction that she might have wished in early 1977, and things would only get worse.

Jennie Hicks was born to Myra and Adrian Cyr on February 6, 1954, in Danbury, Connecticut. Her family moved to Maine when she was a small child, and she started school in the Dixmont School System. She lived in Etna, Maine, a town of under 1,000 people, for much of her young life. As a teenager, she attended Herman High School. The school of about 150 students served a few communities, including Etna and Carmel.[1]

While a freshman, Jennie met James, or Jimmy, Hicks, an older local boy, on their school bus. She passed him a note one day asking him to sit with her. Jimmy complied, and the two began a romantic relationship. Jennie became pregnant at the age of sixteen, and the two decided to marry. According to some sources, Jennie had had some issues with her parents—perhaps only standard teenage issues—and thought that getting married and having a child of her own might gain her some freedom. That would not prove to be the case, however, and her parents apparently did not want the teenager to marry.[2]

The five-foot-seven, blue-eyed, 125-pound, dark blonde–haired young woman did, however, marry Jimmy Hicks. She did so the summer after she met him, in 1970. Jennie dropped out of high school soon thereafter, and the young couple moved in with her parents. Jennie's daughter Abigail* was born in 1973, and Jennie's marriage became an increasingly challenging one. Jimmy finished his senior year of high school and then found a job working at a local woolen mill. He soon moved on to a job with a construction company and joined a labor union. Jennie eventually found work at a local skating rink.[3] Over the years, James Hicks would work a variety of jobs as a union laborer, many of them for Maine paper mills.

At one point, Jimmy Hicks and his father-in-law, Adrian Cyr, worked for the same employer, and the two families moved farther north so that the men would be closer to their jobs. They stayed at the new location for a few years and then returned to the Carmel-Etna area. Both families lived in the area in 1977.[4]

By 1974, the marriage had numerous problems, and the couple applied for a divorce. Jimmy Hicks admitted to numerous instances of sexual infidelity and, according to some sources, had made sexual advances toward Jennie's sister, Denise. Jennie and Jimmy put their divorce proceedings on hold, however, when they discovered that Jennie was pregnant again. She gave birth to her second child, Brian,* in December 1974.[5]

During 1977, the young family lived at the T&N Trailer Park on Route 2 in Carmel. Route 2 was a relatively quiet road on its stretch from Bangor to Newport, passing through Hermon, where the couple had attended high school, and then through Carmel, Etna and eventually Newport. By 1977, Interstate 95 had been constructed through Maine, allowing most through traffic and larger trucks to bypass the narrow, winding Route 2. The stretch of I-95 located between Bangor-Brewer and Newport parallels Route 2. From Newport west, I-95 turns southward, while Route 2 continues predominately westward. Hermon, Carmel and Etna remained small towns

---

* Children's names that appear with an asterisk throughout the book have been changed to protect their identities, although their names have appeared in the press or elsewhere.

in the following years. Newport was the largest community along the Bangor-Newport stretch, but it was still a small town.

The T&N Trailer Park was a relatively small one, with two rows of mobile homes situated fairly close to one another. The Hickses lived in the second row, the one farthest in from Route 2, in the second trailer on the western side of the court, Lot 28. The court featured the single-wide trailers popular at the time—trailers with small rooms and little windows that rolled on a crank. The trailers, with their tiny yards, offered residents little privacy, either from one another or from their next-door neighbors. But it was a place where children could find other kids to play with, and neighbors could talk to one another across their driveways, yards or clotheslines.[6]

Jimmy had secured a job with the Paul Lawrence Construction Co., and he worked that summer at a site in Woodland, Maine, driving for three to four hours each day to make the 115-mile commute. He was out of bed by 4:30 a.m. each day, left the trailer by 5:15 a.m. and started work at 7:30 a.m. Jimmy later said that he made the long commute each day so that he could be with his wife and children, then ages four and two, in the evenings, whereas most of the other men stayed in Woodland during the week.[7]

James and Jennie Hicks lived at the T&N Trailer Court in Carmel at the time of Jennie's disappearance in 1977. The Hickses' trailer has since been destroyed and the trailer park condemned and closed. Jennie and James Hicks would have lived in the second row behind the one shown here. *Photograph by Trudy Irene Scee.*

In addition to baking birthday cakes—some of them quite creative, such as a Greyhound bus cake that Jennie made for her best friend's father—for additional income or as gifts, Jennie had recently started working as a "tray person" or kitchen helper at the Penobscot Nursing Home in Brewer, the "Twin City" to Bangor. She worked a part-time, split-shift position and was considered a dependable, hardworking employee. In order to take the job, she had needed to find a baby sitter. Her friend Linda Elston lived next to Jennie's trailer park and volunteered to baby-sit for her children until Jennie could work out a more permanent arrangement. Jennie was also arranging to start Certified Nursing Assistant (CNA) classes at the nursing home to further her career potential. This would also require child-care arrangements.[8] As with much else in her life, the child-care situation introduced its own problems and mysteries.

Linda Elston lived with her husbands' parents in a small home facing Route 2 in 1977. Her husband, Wayne, was serving in the army. His mother became seriously ill in 1976, and Wayne was transferred to Bangor until after his mother's death. The couple had two daughters. The oldest was the same age as Jennie's daughter Abigail, and their youngest was about the same age as Brian.[9]

Both Wayne and Linda came to know Jennie quite well. Linda considered herself Jennie's best friend. The Elston house was just a two- or three-minute walk from Jennie's trailer, down the short dirt drive in the park and then a few hundred yards along Route 2. "Either I was at her house or she was at mine, every day," mostly when Jimmy was at work, Linda later stated. The two would often go shopping or run other errands with their children. They often went to see Jennie's parents in Newport, especially when her father was ill. Jennie was generally a quiet woman and did not speak of her home life to her friends.[10]

Wayne Elston had known Jimmy Hicks since kindergarten—they were the same age and had gone to the same schools—but Wayne had been friends with Jimmy's brother Sheldon rather than with Jimmy. Sheldon Hicks, like Wayne Elston, had been involved in sports, while Jimmy "pretty much hid himself during school." After he graduated from high school, Jimmy Hicks did not really seem to hang around with any friends; instead, he spent time with his family, in particular his brothers and, of course, his young wife. Wayne and Linda came to know Jimmy better after he moved into the T&N Trailer Park. Of Jennie, Wayne later said, "She was just a very nice person, she would do anything for anyone." Linda said of her, "She was an awesome woman…a mother to die for."[11]

To Wayne, Jennie seemed to be living two or three different lives, "one when she was with other people," one "a good life with her kids" and the third "a terrible life with Jimmy." The marriage clearly had troubles, "but she would never tell anyone what it was all about."[12]

At about the same time as Jennie was looking for a permanent baby sitter, Susan Matley, a fifteen-year-old ward of the State of Massachusetts, ran away from her foster home and hitchhiked to Maine with two of her friends. Dwight Overlock and two other men gave the girls a ride part of the way. Overlock was headed to the Carmel area. When they arrived, Susan—a small and slender girl with blonde hair and blue eyes—decided to stay there with Overlock. Overlock and James Hicks had attended school together but were not close friends.[13]

Overlock's family introduced Jennie to Susan and the two agreed that Susan would move in with Jennie to work as a baby sitter. At the time, Susan described Overlock as her boyfriend.[14]

The teen moved in with the Hicks family. In return for watching the children when Jennie was away, Susan earned her room and board, as well as cigarettes. She slept on the top of a bunk bed in the children's room, while Abigail and Brian slept on the bottom. Jimmy Hicks soon made advances on her. He did so one afternoon while Jennie and the children were away, grabbing and pinching her and backing her into the refrigerator. Susan fled the kitchen. Jimmy followed her and, purposely or not, burned her neck with a cigar after throwing her onto a bed. Susan started crying for him to let her go and he did. Soon thereafter, she told Linda what had happened.[15]

Susan told Jennie about the incident on July 16 or 17, and the married couple argued about it. Jennie, understandably upset about the improper advances on the girl, argued with Jimmy about which one of them—she or her husband—should move out of the mobile home. The two had had similar angry encounters in the past. So far, however, Jimmy had always been able to convince his wife to stay. This time, the situation seemed dire. After all, Jimmy had made advances on a minor in their own home, and Jennie did not let the matter rest.[16]

That Sunday, July 17, Jennie, Jimmy and their little boy went for a long drive. They stopped in the small town of Kenduskeag, and Jennie and Jimmy argued further about the situation. They decided that Jimmy would be the one to leave and that he would be out of the trailer by the end of the month, less than two weeks away. Jennie would keep the kids. Jimmy later said that he thought he would be able to change her mind during the interim. The couple then went home, and on Monday morning, July 18, Jimmy got up as usual and went to work.[17]

Jennie and her children went to see her sister, Denise, that Monday. Denise was living in a nearby town, and after their visit, Jennie headed to Bangor to buy some ingredients to make a cake for Linda Elston's nephew. Abigail, they decided, would stay with Denise. The sisters made plans to meet the next day and for Jennie to take her sister to a dental appointment late in the afternoon. They also talked about the arguments Jennie had had with her husband over the weekend.[18]

Later that Monday, Jennie talked with her friend Linda on the telephone. Jennie told Linda that she had finished making the cake, and they confirmed their plans to take the cake to Bangor the next day. Jennie called again later and asked Linda if she could come over, but Linda said that she could not, as she did not have anyone to watch her children. She would later regret that she had been unable to go.[19]

Jimmy Hicks often troubled Linda. She said later, "We couldn't just sit and talk [when he was around]. She didn't seem to quite dare to say anything." Once when she had tried to visit Jennie in the evening, Hicks had sat there listening and then suddenly announced, "I'll give you a ride home." Jennie, Linda said, just shook her head, as if warning her friend not to get in the car with him. Linda did not.[20]

How Jennie spent the day of July 18 with her children, sister and friend is fairly clear. But from the time James Rodney Hicks returned home that evening, events are far less clear. Different sources tell different stories.

According to Jimmy Hicks's subsequent version of events, the family baby sitter, Susan, had gone out on a date that night with Dwight Overlock. He and Jennie were watching television when Susan returned from her date at about 11:00 p.m. He did not talk to her because he was angry about what she had told Jennie. He said that Jennie did speak to Susan briefly. The couple stayed up a bit longer, talking, and then went to bed. Jennie soon brought Brian into the bed with them, and the three slept together until Jimmy rose to get ready for work in the morning. He drove the family car to work, as he needed to have some repairs made to his truck.[21]

No one saw Jennie Cyr Hicks the next day. At least, none of her friends or adult family members did. No one could say what Jennie did on Tuesday, July 19—if she did anything at all. No one saw Jennie Hicks after July 18; that is, no one who was willing to say that he had. A few people did, however, see her eyeglasses that day. Jenny Cyr Hicks had disappeared, it seemed, without her eyeglasses. Her family and friends never saw her again.[22]

Reports over the next few years placed Jennie in various locations. None of them would ultimately provide a location for the young woman. Police became involved in what soon became an official case, but they could not locate Jennie. It would take over five years to determine, at least partially, what had happened to Jennie. It would take another twenty years to find her.

If you have seen this child, call:
Missing Children Network 1-800-235-3535

1954 Female

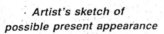

Artist's sketch of possible present appearance

JENNIE HICKS, DOB: 02-06-54. **EYES:** Blue, **HAIR:** Brown, **HEIGHT:** 5'7", **WEIGHT:** 125
I.D. MARKS: Scar behind left ear, two surgical scars on abdomen. Laceration on the scalp.
MEDICAL: Curvature of the spine to the right, fractures of right clavicle & ribs, concussion,
X-rays: Eastern Maine Med. Congenital duplication of the left kidney.
DISAPPEARANCE: On July 19, 1977, after an argument with her husband, Jennie disappeared in the middle of the night from their Carmel, ME, home. Her husband, James, filed a missing persons report, but a real search was never conducted.
Years later, James was charged with the murder of Jennie and was convicted of fourth degree murder by the state of Maine. Throughout the trial, the state failed to produce a body, weapon, motive, bloodstain, sign of the struggle or eyewitness.
Upon the conviction and the sentencing of James Hicks to 10 years in prison, the state issued on July 23, 1985, a death certificate declaring Jennie dead as of July 19, 1977.

Jennie Lynn Cyr Hicks, in an earlier photograph that was distributed widely after her disappearance in 1977 and again in the 1980s, when *Child Keyppers* issued this poster or bulletin describing her. The sketches show what the agency thought Jennie might have looked like in the mid-1980s if she were still alive.

Susan Matley, Jennie's baby sitter, saw Jennie's glasses and her purse at the trailer on July 19 but did not see Jennie. At some point, Susan called Linda and asked her if she knew where Jennie was. Neither thought that anything was seriously wrong at this point, but neither knew where Jennie might be. When Jimmy came home from work, Susan told him that she had not seen Jennie all day. Jimmy then went out to look for his wife and made some telephone calls. He either visited or called the Elston home and then visited Jennie's sister, Denise Clark, her parents, Adrian and Myra Cyr, and finally his own mother, Raye Hicks. He took Brian with him on the last visit. Brian had stayed home with Susan for some of the evening. Abigail was apparently still with Denise. The exact order of James Hicks's visits, and who exactly went with him on which trips, remains unclear. Other details are also in dispute.[23]

Originally, Jimmy Hicks said that Jennie had left her glasses and purse at the trailer. Susan stayed home alone at the trailer for at least a few hours while Hicks purportedly drove around looking for Jennie. When Jimmy stopped at his mother's home, he left Brian with her. Jimmy's brother George left their mother's house with him. After a couple of hours, the brothers supposedly returned to the trailer, picked up Susan and took her to a fair in Bangor. But the major fair in the region, the Bangor State Fair, had not yet started. When the three returned, a light was on inside the mobile home. Jimmy went inside and then came out again, claiming that the glasses were gone. Jimmy Hicks returned to Denise's home later that night and told her that

In 1976 and 1977, Jennie often visited at the Elston house, where her friends Linda and Wayne Elston lived with Wayne's parents and their daughters, Connie and Marion, who played with Jennie's two children. James Hicks came here looking for Jennie after she disappeared. *Photograph by Trudy Irene Scee.*

both Jennie's glasses and her purse were gone—so, he asserted, Jennie must have come back for them while everyone was away. Two people, however, claimed to have seen the missing glasses after July 19, and one of them was a deputy sheriff.[24]

James Rodney Hicks was born on April 17, 1951, in Etna. His family was poor, and his father left the family when Jimmy was a young child. Jimmy supposedly had a rough home life, especially with his mother and some of her friends. He did not move far from his family at any point, except for his construction work, and that was still in central and northern Maine. The trailer he shared with Jennie in 1977 was just a few miles away from his family's Etna property, where he would reside again in the following years with other women.

Twenty-six-year-old Hicks reported his wife missing on July 19. Penobscot County deputy sheriff Timothy Richardson drove from Bangor to the Hickses' home to investigate. Linda and Wayne Elston also reported Jennie missing, as did her family. Exactly who initiated the first report remains unclear, however, as it was either not filed according to regulation or was subsequently lost or destroyed.[25]

Hicks told Richardson that his wife had probably run off with a truck driver. Jennie's parents, however, did not believe this and told the deputy that she would never have run off and left her children behind, nor would she have broken off contact with her entire family.[26] Both parties made repeated attempts—be they half or full hearted, sincere or for show—to look for Jennie.

James Hicks reported that he saw his wife about a week or so after she disappeared, at the Gateway Bar in nearby Newport. The Gateway Bar would later have great significance for Hicks and for another Maine woman. In the meantime, no one could find any evidence that Jennie had actually been at the Gateway in late July 1977. According to Hicks, he had been with his brother George that day, when he saw his wife sitting in a car in front of the Gateway with a tall, dark-haired man. Jennie supposedly told Jimmy that she was staying with this man, a friend of hers, and his parents in Waterville, Maine. She allegedly claimed that she was planning to go to Florida with them in their Winnebago. She inquired about the welfare of her children, or so Hicks claimed.

Other possible "sightings" of Jennie Cyr Hicks occurred. A friend Jennie had known for three or four months, Charlotte Dunifer, supposedly received a call from Jennie about a week after she disappeared. James Hicks also claimed to have heard from his wife at various times, and he told several people about these incidents.

A number of people doubted the words of James Hicks. Hicks had had a reputation for cruelty to animals in his past, and his marriage to Jennie was troublesome. In addition to Jimmy's numerous infidelities, his sexual advances on the couple's baby sitter and their earlier plans to divorce, Jennie and Jimmy had been known to have heated arguments. When the Penobscot County Sheriff's Department looked into the missing persons case, one neighbor told officers that she had overheard a fight between Jennie and James Hicks on July 18, although at the time she reportedly stated that the fight was not any worse than numerous others she had overheard. Susan Matley also stated that Jennie and James Hicks had fought after Jennie went to visit her sister on July 18, but she also said that she had witnessed similar arguments in the past. The last altercation had, however, involved "pushing and shoving."[27]

James Hicks also displayed questionable behavior when he called Jennie's employer and demanded that she release Jennie's last paycheck to him. Although he was informed that that could not happen, Hicks, after yelling over the telephone, showed up at the nursing home the next day. When he was denied the check once again, he swore and said he would be returning with the police.[28]

Myra and Adrian Cyr soon began to suspect that Jimmy had killed their daughter. They confronted James Hicks on a street in Mattwaska, Maine, and accused him of killing Jennie and disposing of her body. They stated that Hicks had replied, "You'll never prove that."[29]

Yet with no direct evidence of a crime, the sheriff's department put the case on the back burner. Little if any further investigation followed in the first weeks after Jennie's disappearance, and for all practical appearances, Jennie had simply vanished. James Hicks moved in with another woman within the year and a second woman within the next year. He soon had another family or families. According to Jennie's family, Hicks kept the son and daughter he had had with Jennie away from them, much to their dismay.

The Cyrs did not give up on their daughter. Although their financial means were limited, they hired a private detective to search for Jennie. With no immediate results from that investigation, Myra Cyr wrote to Maine's secretary of state in February 1978 to enlist his help. She wrote that although she did not know if he was authorized to give her the information she requested, she simply did not know where else to turn. She stated that her daughter had disappeared on July 19, 1977, and they had not heard from her since. "We suspect foul play or self destruction, but the police said that there is no way they can question her husband for fear of being sued for harassment," she stated. Furthermore, she wrote:

Hell Begins

Wayne Elston devoted a wall of his race car shop in Carmel to press clippings and other information about the case of Jennie Lynn Cyr. He also brought exhibits to race car events to keep the word out about the missing woman. Shown here in 2009, the clippings are still in place, with newer ones having been added over the years. On the other side of the aisle, Wayne distributes information about a memorial set up for his daughter, Marion—a friend of Jennie's daughter, Abigail—who died of cancer in the 1980s. *Photograph by Trudy Irene Scee.*

She has two children, a girl seven and a boy three years old and she is a very shy girl who would never leave the house by herself, especially walking like her husband said she did, between 4:00 and 6:00 in the morning with no clothes or pocket book or her glasses. She is nearly blind without her glasses.

What I would like to know is if she renewed her license this year. I realize he could have done it to keep us from looking for her but if she has a new address she would most likely have it on her license.

Myra wrote that Jennie was five feet, six inches tall and weighed about 140 pounds. (Jennie's description varied slightly from previous years, as she may well have gained weight after having two children and leaving behind her teenage years, and the one-inch height variation may have been an error of opinion or perception. Other people described Jennie as being closer to 140 pounds than 125 in 1977.) Myra Cyr did not know her daughter's Social Security number or her driver's license number, but she pleaded:

I am her mother and very concerned about her whereabouts. If you can tell me if she has renewed her license and the change of address, I would very much appreciate it. At least I would know she was alright and perhaps someday she will come back.

Myra signed her name and gave her address.[30] Myra's letter would one day become part of a full-scale investigation into Jennie's whereabouts.

Myra Cyr did not find out where her daughter had gone. But she waited. Then, five years after Jennie disappeared, another woman vanished. Another woman who had lived in the same area of Maine. Another woman who had encountered James Rodney Hicks.

CHAPTER TWO

HISTORY ALMOST REPEATS ITSELF

The Case of Jerilyn Leigh Towers

Jerilyn Leigh Towers turned thirty-four in 1981. A Maine native, she was born on December 2, 1947, and was raised in Rome. She had three children she was attempting to raise by herself, although two of them were primarily staying with her daughter's father. She lived in one side of a duplex on Marginal Way in Newport in the autumn of 1982; her mother and stepfather lived on the other side. She had three sisters and two brothers. She also had a boyfriend who was currently in jail, and she was in the process of ending that relationship. Jerilyn liked to bowl and play cribbage, she sometimes went camping and she always kept a penny in her shoe for luck.[31]

Jerilyn or Jeri was last seen at the Gateway Lounge or Bar in Newport, Maine, on October 16, 1982. It was a Saturday evening, and her stepfather had dropped her off at the bar at about 6:30 p.m. Jerilyn had gone bowling during the day and wanted to have a few drinks and relax. Her stepfather waited at home watching television, expecting to pick Jerilyn up again later that night. The call to come and get her never arrived. A vehicle with a loud exhaust did pull into their driveway at about 1:00 a.m., and the driver turned off the headlights. Mr. Tibbetts shut off the television, and the couple went to sleep, as they figured someone was dropping their daughter off. That proved not to be the case, however. Jerilyn did not come home that night; nor would she return in the days and weeks to follow.[32]

The next day, Jerilyn's eldest son went over to his grandparents' side of the building and told them that his mother had not come home. His grandparents became alarmed because they had not heard from Jerilyn, she had had only six dollars on her and she was taking prescription drugs for a liver problem and did not have her medicine with her. Jerilyn had recently been hospitalized, and her health remained shaky.[33]

Jerilyn's mother, June Tibbetts, contacted the Newport police on October 18, 1982, to inform them that her daughter had not been seen since October 16. Officer James Ricker responded to the call. June Tibbetts told Ricker that her daughter had gone off for short periods of time in the past but that she had always let someone know where she was. This time, she had not contacted anyone. The Tibbettses had decided to run a notice in the local papers asking anyone who might have seen Jerilyn to contact them, and they had already received one response. A "fortuneteller" had called to inform the family that he believed that Jerilyn was in a river in Bingham. Police gave the call no credence.[34]

More disturbing, perhaps, than the communication from the so-called psychic was the fact that Ricker could locate no one who admitted to having seen Jerilyn after her father had dropped her off at the Gateway on October 16. Ricker issued a missing persons report, including a complete description of Jerilyn.[35]

When last seen, the five-foot-six, 200-pound, brown-eyed, dark-haired Jeri had been wearing black slacks and a blue-checkered button-up shirt. She also had on sturdy Maine Dexter shoes and her trademark men's tube socks. She wore a gold, double-banded mother's ring set with red, yellow, blue and green stones. She had four stones because, although she was raising three children, she had a fourth child who was dearly loved and being raised by a family member. Jeri's hair was fairly short at the time and was described as "salt and pepper." Her weight was above normal for her because of her health issues.[36]

Corporal Eugene Robinson soon joined Ricker on the case. Two days after Ricker began the investigation into Jerilyn's disappearance, Robinson was contacted by Nathan Small, a dowser from Skowhegan and the same person who had contacted the Tibbetts family. Small claimed that he had a special ability to locate the bodies of missing people. He said that he believed that Jerilyn Towers was dead and her body was floating in the river in Bingham, temporarily trapped by some rocks. Although the officer did not think Small's claims were legitimate, the man had given an exact location for a body, and Robinson felt that he had to follow up on the call. The Somerset County sheriff, within whose jurisdiction the supposed location of the body lay, already had a plane in the air, and although he also doubted Small's credibility, he had the pilot check the specified location. No body was found.[37]

Over the following days and months, more information was gleaned about the last known days of Jerilyn Towers. Her mother, June, and her stepfather, Millard, had brought Jerilyn and her three children—Raymond, Thomas

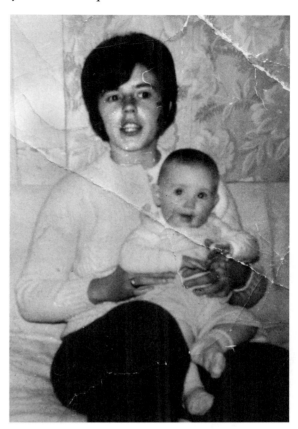

Jerilyn Towers as a young mother, a happier time for her, shown here in the early 1970s. Although she was often separated from one or more of her children, at the time she disappeared, she remained in close contact with them all. *Photograph courtesy of Tammy Price.*

and Tammy—to the Pittsfield Bowling Alley during the afternoon of October 16. The day was to be something of a family reunion or celebration. Before that day, the two younger children, Thomas and Tammy, had been living with Tammy's father in the Skowhegan area. He had brought the two kids to visit Jerilyn in Newport only the night before.[38]

June Tibbetts stayed in the car while the others went into the bowling alley. Her husband and Jerilyn enjoyed a drink while the children started bowling. Millard Tibbetts came back to the car after a short while to tell June that Jerilyn had forgotten to bring her money with her and wanted him to go back to their house to get it. According to her parents, Jeri had been saving up her change in a mayonnaise jar so that she could pay for this day of bowling with her children. As she had only Aid to Dependant Children and food stamps with which to support her children, saving up any amount of money was deemed a feat for her. Millard went to retrieve the money and returned later in the afternoon. Jeri and the kids counted out enough change to pay the bowling tab. The entire family then left the alley. Tammy, however, later said that her mother had spent her bowling money on drinks, and that she (Tammy), a regular bowler in the area, had felt angry and humiliated when her mother had to send for her change and made the children count it out.[39]

By all accounts, Jerilyn had been drinking that afternoon, and she decided to stop for a drink at the Gateway Lounge when the family returned to Newport. The Tibbettses let Jerilyn out at the bar, and she told her stepfather that she would call him later for a ride home. The family watched her enter the Gateway and then went home.[40]

The Tibbettses went to their part of the duplex and the children to theirs. Raymond, the oldest child, was fifteen at the time, and this was apparently not his first time watching his siblings. June went to bed before her husband——perhaps tired from her work every week taking care of her daughter Margaret, who had advanced-stage multiple sclerosis. Millard stayed up watching *Stacy's Country Jamboree*, as he often did on Saturday nights, until he heard the vehicle later that night. June was still awake, and

Jerilyn Towers disappeared after leaving the Gateway Lounge in Newport in 1982. Although the establishment has since been renamed and made into a restaurant, the building has changed little since the 1980s. *Photograph by Trudy Irene Scee.*

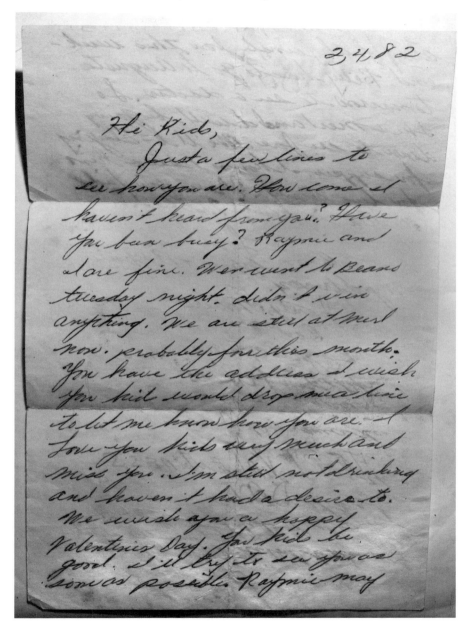

Although she was sometimes separated from one or more of her children in the mid-1970s, she always kept in contact with them, sending them "chatty" letters about everyday events. She often signed her full name to her letters and provided her current address as well. *Letter courtesy of Tammy Price.*

they both thought that Jeri had found a ride home from the Gateway. It was Raymond who came into his grandparents' home the next morning to tell them that his mother had not returned. The family then contacted the Newport police.[41]

Something of a break came a few days after the self-proclaimed psychic contacted the police. Bonnie Willey called the Newport police and told them that she had seen Jerilyn's photograph in the local newspaper and recognized her. She said that she had seen Jerilyn at the Gateway on October 16 and that Jerilyn had seemed depressed. Jerilyn had recently received a letter from her boyfriend, and the two were having problems, hence her depression.[42]

Jerilyn's boyfriend was incarcerated at the time at the Somerset County Jail. Jerilyn had visited him regularly, the last time just four days before her disappearance. Robinson made inquiries about her visitation dates and who had accompanied her on the visits.[43] Officer Robinson also pursued another angle—he contacted James Rodney Hicks.

Robinson had received an anonymous phone message in October stating that a man named Gary Hicks was the last person seen with Jerilyn Towers at the Gateway before she disappeared. Robinson went to the bar to follow up on the message, although he did not know anyone by that name—nor did anyone else. However, he did find James Hicks at the bar.[44]

Hicks was living in Etna at the time, on his family's property. When questioned by Robinson in mid-November, he replied that he did not know Jerilyn Towers or anything about her disappearance. Robinson spoke with him for a half hour. It seemed that Hicks was being straight with him and, indeed, that he was being quite cooperative. Hicks said that he had not been at the bar on October 16 and "that he had never left the Gateway with any woman." (He had, however, he said, had sexual relations at about that time with an unknown woman in the lounge's restroom.) Hicks also said that he did not know anything about a Gary Hicks. Robinson decided that the call was unfounded.[45] He would soon learn that it was not.

Although James Hicks claimed not to have been at the Gateway Lounge on October 16, the bartender on duty that night told a few people, after the fact, that she remembered Hicks having been there. The bartender, Judy Hopkins, had previously told police that she did not know if Hicks had been in the bar that night.[46]

Robinson followed up on this rumor and talked to the people with whom Judy Hopkins had spoken. They confirmed what he had heard. On November 20, Officer Ricker met with Judy Hopkins, and Hopkins confirmed the information that the police had received about Hicks being in the bar on October 16. Hopkins stated that Hicks had indeed been at the Gateway that night—he had come in at about 10:00 p.m. and, for at least part of the night, had sat at a corner of the bar drinking with Jerilyn. He had paid for their drinks. Judy described Hicks as being about five feet, eight inches tall and weighing around 150 pounds. He had a beard and was wearing a Stihl chainsaw cap. She said that Towers and Hicks had left the bar together, but she did not know if they had gotten into a vehicle together. She said that she had honestly not remembered Hicks as having been there until he came in again on November 17. Even then, she had not been certain if his name was Gary or James Hicks. She remembered faces and drinking choices better than she did names. Hicks had consumed bottled Miller beer when he came in November, just as he had in October, and he wore the same yellow cap with the Stihl logo.[47]

Ricker subsequently contacted the Etna postmaster, Richards Mills, to ask if he had a street address for Hicks. Mills replied that he knew Hicks personally and found him to be rather "strange" and said that Hicks's first wife had disappeared five years previously, never to be heard from again. He and everyone else he knew, Mills stated, believed that Hicks had murdered

Shown here in the year before she vanished, Jerilyn Towers used her ID card in lieu of a driver's license, as she did not drive. The photograph used on her ID was often used, in the press and elsewhere, in the years following her disappearance. *Courtesy of Tammy Price.*

his wife and then filed a missing persons report. Mills then described the physical location of Hicks's home.[48] The hunt was on.

Officers Ricker and Robinson drove to Hicks's home and found him standing by the front door. One of the officers informed him that they wanted to ask him some questions in reference to a missing persons case, and Hicks voluntarily entered the police car. The officers attempted to inform Hicks of his rights, as they believed he was lying when he responded to their initial questions, but he kept interrupting them, talking about how he knew why they were there—that everybody thought he had murdered his first wife. The police were finally, after numerous interruptions, able to finish reading Hicks his Miranda rights, and Hicks said that he understood them.[49]

The police interview continued, and Hicks asked if he could go in the house to get a drink of water. He said he thought that he would faint otherwise. He appeared extremely nervous and was sweating profusely and stuttering. The three men went into the house. Hicks sat in a chair and then rose to get a glass of water. He sat back down, prepared to take a drink and then poured the water all over himself. His voice or attention faded in and out during the questioning that followed, and he seemed to have fainted at one juncture. He told the officers that he *might* have been at the Gateway on October 16 and, eventually, that he *might* have been talking to Jerilyn Towers that night, as he often talked to women in bars. He thought he had stayed until the bar closed. When informed that witnesses had seen him leave with Jerilyn, he stared at the policemen and then said that maybe he had walked out at the same time as some girl, "but he did not *think* that they were together." He then acted confused and said he felt too much pressure, that he felt the same way he had felt when questioned after his wife disappeared. But, he said, he knew his wife Jennie was alive because he had seen her two weeks after she had left their house; he said that she sent Christmas presents to their children every year and that her parents had had contact with her since she left. Hicks then stated that *if* he had been at the bar on October 16, he had stayed until closing time and had woken up at the Etna campgrounds at 4:30 a.m. The officers ascertained that his car, registered to his girlfriend, had had a bad exhaust, which had since been repaired. The officers asked him why his vehicle had been sighted at 2:00 a.m. on Towers's street. Again, he stared at the two police officers.[50]

A later communication stated that at the time of the interview, "Hicks was suspected of nothing other than a 'fling' with a girl he had met in a bar." Hicks's current live-in girlfriend, Linda Marquis, had come home at the end of the interview, however, and "kicked" the police out of the house. As Ricker explained in 2009, "She asked us to leave and we left. I was trying to be discreet, but she knew that there was something going on about a woman."

Hicks, he said, had started shaking the moment he asked him where he had let Jerilyn Towers off that night. As police followed up on other leads, their suspicions of Hicks only deepened.[51]

Unable to reach Jennie's parents immediately, the police decided to speak with Jennie's uncle, Claude Cyr, and his family at their Carmel home. The members of Jennie's family present that day insisted that Jennie had *not* been seen or heard from by the family since July 18, 1977. Furthermore, one of the women, Susan Hart, said that Jennie had told her that if something ever went wrong with her marriage, she would never leave her two children behind. She had, however, left the children, her glasses and all of her clothing behind when she disappeared. The incident with the baby sitter also came to light, as Jennie had told her sister that Jimmy was trying to get the girl to have sex with him. Police at that time did not know the baby sitter's name.[52]

Robinson was then able to speak with Jennie Cyr's mother, who told him that when she had accused Hicks of killing Jennie, he had answered, "You'll never prove it." She said that Jennie and Jimmy had had numerous fights and that on a couple of occasions Jennie had been hospitalized. Jennie was also, she said, treated for various other injuries, injuries she thought that Hicks had deliberately inflicted on her daughter. Police requested Jennie's medical records.[53]

Yet neither the person nor the body of Jerilyn Towers was to surface in the upcoming weeks or months, nor, in spite of renewed scrutiny, would that of Jennie Cyr Hicks. Law enforcement did, however, investigate Hicks and his movements, both past and recent, as closely as possible.

Without sufficient evidence to indict James Hicks for any crime against Jerilyn Towers, law enforcement decided to explore how strong a case might be built against Hicks for the disappearance of his wife and with what crime he might be charged. The Maine State Police—which has jurisdiction over all murders in Maine except those occurring in Bangor, Portland and Lewiston—began a series of interviews with possible witnesses.

After locating the young woman, Detective Richard Reitchell of the Maine State Police (MSP) interviewed Susan Matley, the former baby sitter for the Hicks children, about her relationship with the family and what she had witnessed in 1977. Matley had married in the intervening years and had recently returned to Massachusetts. Reitchell interviewed her in Perperill, Massachusetts, in December 1982. Although he noted that Susan seemed to be confused in places and had forgotten a bit over the years, she did relate specific events of that July. She said that when she returned from her date with Dwight Overlock at about 4:00 a.m. on July 19, she saw Jennie in the living room wearing a blue bathrobe. Jennie did not say anything to her, and James Hicks told her that Jennie was asleep.[54]

Susan said that she "got real bad vibes" when she saw Jennie and that Hicks seemed upset and acted "very, very peculiar." Susan did not see any blood, but she did think that she later heard some sort of noise outside and a door opening. She did not hear a car start.[55]

Reitchell also interviewed Trudy Levansaller in December. Although she had since moved, Levansaller had been the Hickses' next-door neighbor when Jennie disappeared. Levansaller told the detective that she had seen Jennie with black eyes and a bruise on her thigh. She also said she had seen Hicks chasing Susan Matley around the trailer. She stated that on the last night anyone had seen Jennie, she had heard her yelling, and at one point Jennie had screamed, "Stop. Please stop. You are going to kill me." Furthermore, about one week after Jennie disappeared there had been severe septic problems in the trailer park, especially near their lots.[56]

The MSP interviewed other people, in particular other neighbors. A couple of children supposedly told older members of their family that they had heard screams on the night Jennie disappeared, but their memories were less clear by 1982. A relative of Dwight Overlock reported that he had seen Susan with a black eye at some point after Jennie had disappeared, and he thought that James Hicks had done something to both women.[57]

One particular person of interest in terms of the information that she could provide was Fern Godsoe, one of Hicks's girlfriends. Fern, a few years younger than Hicks, told police in early February 1983 at her home in Gilman's Trailer Park in Newport that she had been with Hicks for some time. She had started dating him not long after Jennie had gone missing and had been in a relationship with Hicks for well over a year.[58]

While Fern Godsoe was with him, Hicks had remodeled the trailer he had shared with Jennie. Fern stated that she did not know why Hicks had redone the mobile home, as it already looked pretty good to her. Hicks gave her his furniture and then sold the trailer. He gave his marital mattress and box springs to his mother, but both ended up going to the dump. Godsoe had seen the mattress and said that there was "a great big bloodstain on the mattress that was about eighteen inches in diameter." Either James or his mother had explained that at some point in their marriage, Jimmy and Jennie had been arguing and Jennie had either fallen or he had hit her, and somehow she cut her back. Fern thought that the fight had had something to do with their daughter Abigail. James Ricker later stated that Fern had wanted to get rid of the mattress, no matter the source of the blood. Fern had been living or staying at the trailer with Hicks, and as he initially refused to get rid of the blood-soaked mattress, they had slept on it together.[59]

Fern, upon inquiry, said that she had had a normal sex life with Hicks. However, he was often rough, including when she was very pregnant with her daughter Catherine.* They had had other problems as well.[60]

Hicks moved in with Fern after he sold the trailer in Carmel. She said of Hicks, "Jim is manly. He swears and cusses a lot." She said that she did not know anything about any interaction between Hicks and Jerilyn Towers. She also said that she did not think that Hicks had been very close to his brothers—he was a man to whom it was hard to get close.[61] He was also apparently a hard man to get away from.

Law enforcement presented the above and other evidence to the state. Determining whether there was sufficient evidence to bring a case against Hicks fell to the Office of the Attorney General of Maine. At the time, James Tierney was serving as Maine's attorney general.

The criminal division of the attorney general's office had become involved with the James Hicks case after the disappearance of Jerilyn Towers, as had the Maine State Police. The combined agencies, along with the Newport police, determined that when Jennie Lynn Hicks disappeared, law enforcement had conducted a "botched investigation." William Stokes

James Hicks spent time with his girlfriend, Fern Godsoe, at Gilman's Trailer Court in Newport after his wife Jennie disappeared. He later remodeled and sold his trailer in Carmel, gave Fern some of his furniture and lived with her for a time. *Photograph by Trudy*

of the attorney general's office was only thirty-three years old when he first became involved in the case and was relatively new to the criminal division. Police, he said, "never investigated [the Jennie Lynn Cyr case] as a homicide or even a missing persons, they accepted Hicks's story that she had left."[62] The Penobscot County deputy sheriff who had initially investigated the case had failed to follow up, and the state essentially had to start over.

Jennie Cyr's family had never accepted Hicks's story. When James Ricker started reinvestigating the case in 1982, their reaction was unforgettable. "I can't even describe the excitement of the Cyr family," he said. "It was all bottled up in them. 'Why hasn't anyone listened to us?' was their reaction. It was just unbelievable." Some of the people who became involved with James Hicks were, for lack of a better word, "victims of society." The case was not more rigorously pursued, Ricker believed, "because of the type of people they were." To some, they simply seemed like "the kind of people who would leave." But Jennie Lynn Cyr had not been that kind of woman.[63]

Over the following months and years, James Hicks would come to hate James Ricker. Ricker stated in 2009 that "[Hicks] despised me because I'm the one who told him that he was guilty. I would never, *ever* give him any peace...I didn't harass him, but I never, ever played the 'good cop' with him."[64] Ricker hounded James Hicks for twenty years about what had become of Jennie Cyr and Jerilyn Towers, and he eventually added his weight to yet another investigation.

Ricker believed that on that day at the Hicks residence in Etna, when police had gone to ask Hicks about Jerilyn Towers, Hicks had been about to break down and confess his crime or crimes. Then Linda Marquis showed up and insisted that the officers leave. "The first time I interviewed him, the only time I interviewed him, I almost had him. He was about to break down. I know he was," Ricker later stated.[65]

Hicks had not broken down to the point of making a confession, however. The state still had only circumstantial evidence in the case of Jennie Lynn Cyr and no strong evidence at all in the case of Jerilyn Leigh Towers. Jennie had been married to James Hicks and had suddenly disappeared, with no evidence that she had done so of her own volition, and testimony existed of a tumultuous relationship between the two. Still, no body had ever been recovered. Were the case to go to trial, and were a jury to convict Hicks without a body, it would be a historic event or development.

Yet the only evidence that the state had regarding Jerilyn Towers and James Hicks, according to Bill Stokes, was that "they were in the bar together." In light of the difficulty of establishing that case, Stokes stated, "we focused our attention on Jennie Cyr."[66]

History Almost Repeats Itself

Law enforcement and the state wanted to prosecute James Hicks for the death of his wife, but did they have enough evidence in 1983 to do so? The state decided that it would prosecute. Fernand (Fern) R. LaRochelle, as chief of the criminal division of the attorney general's office, led the prosecution.

As Bill Stokes described it, "Fern came to me, and laid out the case. I wrote the memo—it was designed to get past the *corpus* selection rule—to prove that the crime was committed. We had no body." In such cases, 1) the state had to prove that a crime had been committed and 2) before using a statement by the defense (such as a confession), the state had to show that a crime had been committed. Rather confusing criteria, perhaps, but together they were meant to ensure that in a case without a body the prosecution had more evidence than a confession.[67]

Stokes wrote the memo for LaRochelle, who in turn presented it to the presiding judge. The judge initially seemed a bit skeptical. But then "Fern came back and said that after he read the memo…the judge's facial expression changed. He told the prosecution, 'If you can present the evidence, then I think it will get to a jury.'"[68]

CHAPTER THREE

JUSTICE ALMOST SERVED

James Rodney Hicks Goes to Jail

T he Maine Attorney General's Office presented its case against James Hicks to the Penobscot Grand Jury in Bangor, and on October 4, 1983, the jury determined that "on or about the nineteenth day of July, 1977… James Hicks did cause the death of Jennie Hicks, intending to cause her death or knowing that her death would almost certainly result from his conduct."[69]

Police arrested James Hicks for homicide that same day. He was arraigned before Judge Herbert T. Silsby II on October 7, and, as he was found indigent, the court appointed him counsel. Hicks pleaded not guilty. On November 8, Hicks had a change of counsel. Hicks's new attorney filed pretrial motions, and a hearing for these was held on January 5, 1984. Jury selection started on March 12, and the trial commenced immediately thereafter. Marshall Stern and J. Hillary Billings of Bangor represented Hicks at trial. Billings, a younger associate at the time, took the lead role for the defense. Fernand LaRochelle led the prosecution team.[70]

At the time of his trial, Hicks was in a relationship with Linda Marquis. The two had two children together, David* and Evelyn*, the youngest little more than a baby at the time of Hicks's arrest. Jennie's children, Abigail and Brian, also lived with them, as did two of Linda's children from a previous relationship. Marquis and Hicks had reportedly met about a year after Jennie Hicks disappeared and had lived together on the Hicks family homestead in Etna since 1978. Hicks's affairs with Linda Marquis and Fern Godsoe apparently had significant overlap.[71]

When James Hicks went to trial in 1984 for the death of his wife, Jennie Lynn Cyr Hicks, the State of Maine had never convicted a person for homicide without the evidence of a body. The burden of proof on the part of the prosecution would be heavy, and the trial would be based largely on circumstantial evidence. The state listed twenty-two witnesses for the

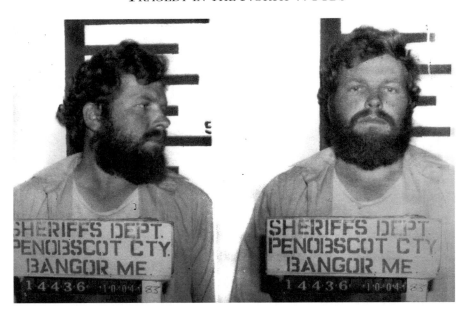

In 1983, James Hicks was arrested for the murder of his wife, Jennie Cyr Hicks, in 1977. Hicks would make additional appearances at the Penobscot County Jail in subsequent years. *Courtesy of Penobscot County Sheriff's Department.*

prosecution. The defense listed a large number of witnesses also, including Penobscot County deputy sheriff Timothy Richardson.

Testimony presented at the trial went beyond that initially received by investigating officers. Legal documents and items such as Myra Cyr's 1978 letter to the secretary of state were introduced. Stories of supposed sightings of Jennie were recited. Supposed facts were vigorously contested by both the prosecution and defense.[72]

Trudy Levansaller testified that she had lived next to the Hicks family for about a year, during which time she had overheard a number of arguments. On the night that Jennie went missing, she was awakened by screams coming from the Hicks trailer. She heard a man yelling and screaming obscenities. She also heard Jennie yelling either "Oh, stop Jimmy, please stop" or "Stop, you're killing me!" Then, except for the sound of a child crying, all was silent. Eventually, Trudy heard something else. She heard what sounded like "someone…sawing wood and chopping wood inside of a trailer." She was not able to go back to sleep that night, but she claimed that she had not heard anyone coming or going.[73]

Shortly after dawn, according to Levansaller's testimony, Hicks had backed his pickup truck up to the front door of the trailer. He had cement blocks, chains and a cooler in the back of the truck. Levansaller said that Hicks asked her later in the day if she had seen Jennie. He said that Jennie was gone but her glasses and purse were still in the trailer. On cross-examination, Trudy admitted that she had not actually seen the source of some of the noises she heard and that her earlier testimony with Deputy Richardson, now Sheriff Richardson, was probably more accurate in details. Sheriff Richardson testified that when he had originally spoken with Levansaller, she had stated that the July 18 fight was not worse than earlier ones, and she had not told him that she had heard Jennie yelling. Nor had she mentioned seeing or hearing Hicks's truck backing up to the trailer the next morning.

Another neighbor, Ruth Purvis, who had lived on the other side of the Hickses in 1977, testified that she had not heard anything that night. Nor had she heard any serious arguments before then.

Levansaller testified that she had previously seen bruises and black eyes on Jennie and that Jennie had told her that they had been caused by James Hicks. However, two of Jennie's friends during the months before she died—Linda Elston and Charlotte Dunifer—said that they had not seen the bruises or any other injuries. Linda, Jennie's close friend, did not remember Jennie ever telling her that her husband hit her. Levansaller, however, insisted that she had heard physical fights at the trailer several times.

Susan Matley Brennon, who had been in the Hickses' home during the night of the alleged homicide, gave detailed testimony as to what she had seen and heard. In addition to her initial reports to law enforcement, Susan said that before she had gone out on her date with Dwight Overlock on July 18, 1977, she had witnessed a disagreement between James and Jennie Hicks at dinner. James Hicks told her that they would discuss why Jennie was upset later. When she came home early in the morning of July 19, Jennie and James were in the living room, in front of the television. She recalled:

> *I opened the door and seen Jimmy sitting down in the chair and Jenny* [sic] *was laying down on the love seat and I asked him, I said, is Jennie asleep? And he said, yes. How was your night? And I said, fine. And I walked into the bathroom and then I climbed up on top of the top bunk, the bed, and I was scared, nervous, I was listening.*

When asked why she had been afraid, Susan said, "Things didn't seem right." Jennie was wearing her blue bathrobe and laying down on the loveseat, and "her feet were scrunched up and her head was like, one eye and half of her nose and her hair was more or less covering her face." Jennie's arms "were kind of like in different weird positions. She was in an uncomfortable position."

Upon his 1983 arrest for the murder of Jennie Lynn Cyr Hicks, James Hicks was held at the Penobscot County Jail while awaiting trial. This would not be his last incarceration at the facility. As shown here, the jail, on the right, is connected to the Penobscot Sheriff's Department and is situated next to and behind the Penobscot County Courthouse, located to the left. *Photograph by Trudy Irene Scee.*

On cross-examination, Susan reiterated her earlier testimony to police that she had not seen any blood, broken furniture or anything else disturbed. But, she noted, she had not been looking for that sort of thing. She could not swear that Jennie had not actually been sleeping, as James Hicks had told her she was.

The Hickses' former baby sitter also testified that after she had gone into the children's bedroom, she had heard noises like scuffing slippers on the floor, like someone in slippers being dragged, and the sound of a door opening. She was afraid to get up and see what was going on. She had buried her head under the covers and eventually fell asleep. The next thing she remembered hearing was Brian Hicks waking up and crying in the doorway of his parents' bedroom. Jennie was not in the trailer. Susan did not remember the time. She acknowledged that the telephone might have rung while she was asleep, or something else might have happened, as she was, she admitted, a heavy sleeper. She also could not swear that Jennie was not in the home when she had heard the earlier noises in the night or early morning. She stated again that Jennie's purse and glasses were on the kitchen table that day, and that the truck was in the driveway. She had called Linda Elston to inquire where Jennie might have gone, and she recalled that Jennie's fuzzy blue bathrobe, which Jennie had been wearing when Susan returned from her date, was missing. James Hicks later testified that his wife had never owned such a bathrobe.

Fern Godsoe testified that she had lived with James Hicks for about eighteen months after Jennie disappeared and said that she still had the loveseat or couch that James Hicks had given her. She had lain on it and confirmed that sleeping on it was indeed possible. Testimony was also presented that Susan Matley had once told James Hicks's mother, Raye, and his sister, Starr, that when she came home that night, James and Jennie were both awake and acting very angry. She had allegedly taken Brian from the room and put him to bed.

As for Jennie's glasses, while Susan testified that Jennie had very poor eyesight and definitely needed her glasses, Denise Clark, Jennie's sister, stipulated that sometimes Jennie chose not to wear them. But Denise reasserted that Jennie had told her that if James did not move out of the trailer, she would, and she would take her children with her. Regardless of whether Jennie sometimes left the house without her glasses, or whether her glasses were in the kitchen on the day of July 19, Susan told the jury that Jennie's glasses had been in the trailer on the evening of July 19. When Susan returned from a fair with the Hicks brothers, James went inside and said that the glasses were missing. He concluded that Jennie must have come back to get them. Furthermore, two witnesses testified that they saw Jennie's glasses *after* the date of her disappearance. (James Hicks later stated that Jennie had an old pair of glasses, as well as the ones she primarily wore, and perhaps those were the ones seen after she disappeared.)

James Hicks's mother testified, among other things, that her son George had not been at her house on the night of July 18. He did not show up there until days after Jennie disappeared. Thus, Susan Matley's testimony that the three of them had gone to a fair that night could not be true.

James Hicks took the stand at his trial and insisted that he and Jennie had indeed been watching television when Susan returned from her date that night. He said she returned at about 11:00 p.m., as that was the curfew Jennie had given the girl. He said that he had not spoken with Susan when she came home because he was angry with her for telling Jennie that he had made sexual overtures to her. Yet he asserted that he had had discussions, even arguments, with Jennie in the past about his infidelity and that Susan had only added fuel to the fire. He had thought he would be able to persuade Jennie to stay with him, just as he had in the past. He said that Jennie had talked to Susan briefly that night when she returned from her date. He and

One of Bangor's oldest buildings, the Penobscot County Courthouse served as the scene of Hicks's murder trial in 1984. *Photograph by Trudy Irene Scee.*

Jennie had then gone to bed, he testified, and soon thereafter Jennie had brought Brian in to join them. James Hicks said that he got up and went to work as usual in the morning. His wife was still in bed. He and Jennie had already discussed her taking the truck to a mechanic that day to have the wheels realigned, so he drove the car. Furthermore, he testified, a friend of Jennie's had received a call after her disappearance from someone claiming to be Jennie. The caller asked for James Hicks to bring her some of her clothing. (The woman who received the call, Charlotte Dunifer, however, testified that she had not told Hicks about the call, nor had Linda Elston, whom she had told.) James Hicks stated that he did not kill his wife and that he was certain that she was alive after her disappearance.

The prosecution concluded its case on March 20. The defense moved for a motion of acquittal. It was denied, and the defense presented its witnesses. On March 22, the defense's presentation concluded, and it again asked for a motion of acquittal. The court again denied it, and Justice Browne gave his instructions to the jury. The jury adjourned at 1:05 p.m. and returned at 3:15 p.m. to ask that certain testimony be read back to it. It again returned at 9:30 p.m., with the same request regarding other testimony, and asked for instructions on the difference between second- and fourth-degree homicide. At 10:25 p.m., the jury returned for the final time.[74]

Justice Almost Served

The jury did not believe James Rodney Hicks. After deliberating for nine hours, on March 22, 1984, it found Hicks guilty of homicide in the fourth degree. This was the first known jury in Maine history to convict a defendant on a homicide without the evidence of a body. The court scheduled sentencing for April 20, and on that day, Justice Robert L. Browne sentenced thirty-three-year-old Hicks to ten years of incarceration, the maximum sentence for fourth-degree murder. Maine's criminal code had been revised since 1977—some classes of homicide were eliminated, and the older, fourth-degree murder charge was considered comparable to the current manslaughter charge.

According to one juror, testimony presented at the trial did indeed show that Jennie Hicks was not someone who would abandon her children. "We thought he was guilty, and we were right," the juror, who wishes to remain nameless, stated. The juror did not discuss any specifics of the deliberations but said in 2009 that after the verdict many people were appalled that Hicks had been found guilty and sentenced without a body. Judge Browne received criticism for the sentencing, and some people questioned the wisdom of Marshall Sterns, who let Billings handle the defense. Sterns was much more experienced, and some people felt certain that he would have been able to win the case. Billings had seemed rather pompous to some of the jurors, while Timothy Richardson, the deputy who had first investigated the case, "was adamant about what he said. The attitude came across that this [the case of Jennie Cyr going missing] was a trivial matter to him." In addition, at one point, one of the exhibits—visible just behind him—conflicted directly with his description of the Hicks trailer. On top of that, James Hicks seemed extremely cold and dispassionate about what had happened to his wife.[75]

According to Bill Stokes, "We always theorized that with the neighbor hearing the screaming, and the baby sitter's testimony [along with other testimony]…the jury figured that they had argued and he had hit her and panicked. So, they acquitted him of murder because they did not think it was premeditated."[76]

J. Hillary Billings and the firm of Sterns & Goldsmith contested Hicks's homicide conviction. They served a notice of appeal on April 20, 1984, the day of Hicks's sentencing. At the outset of their appeal, they asserted:

> *To state that the facts of this case were unusual would be the height of understatement. It would be easy to defend the position that a verdict of guilty in the charge of homicide has never, in the history of American jurisprudence, been returned on scantier evidence of death.*[77]

This was a bit of an exaggeration, perhaps, but the conviction was a historic one for the state. And the state, the appeal argued, presented far less evidence than it needed to support such a conviction. According to the appellant's attorneys:

> *The State presented no evidence at trial of a deceased victim's body nor was there any direct evidence that a death had occurred. There was no evidence of a murder weapon. There were no bloodstains or bloodstained clothes. There was no testimonial evidence of striking or hitting. There was no evidence of violent conduct, or for that matter, any conduct whatsoever by the defendant. There was no scientific evidence of the alleged scene of the alleged crime. There was no tangible or physical evidence of a struggle nor were there any statements entered into evidence of a struggle, nor were there any statements entered into the evidence at trail attributing to the Defendant which may in any manner be considered confession to criminal wrongdoing. Trial took place almost seven years after the events alleged in the indictment.*

The appeal reviewed the trial testimony and pointed out some of the shortcomings or inconsistencies of that testimony. The defense pointed out, for example, the disparity in the various accounts of the events at the Hicks trailer on July 18 and early on July 19, 1977. Some testimony varied markedly, not only from testimony from other witnesses, but also from earlier testimony provided by the same witness. One example, and perhaps the most marked one, was the evidence provided by Hicks's neighbor Trudy Levansaller. Levansaller had described events or sounds at the trailer that, according to the defense attorneys, "conjures images from the writing of Stephen King or Alfred Hitchcock." Yet neighbor Ruth Purvis had not heard anything during those same hours. Furthermore, Levansaller provided details at the trial that she had not provided just after Jennie's disappearance—five days after it, as given to the deputy sheriff—and those details stood "in marked contrast to her trial testimony." Information provided by her to Maine State Police detective Ralph Holmes several months after Jennie's disappearance also did not include the horrors that Levansaller described at trial. Detective Holmes had seen James Hicks just a few minutes after he spoke with Levansaller that day, and he had seen no reason to speak with him.

As for later events, the defense argued, "It is virtually impossible to reconcile the various accounts of the Defendant's travels on the night of Jennie's disappearance." Furthermore, logistics made the "Defendant's alleged travels a practical impossibility. Someone, or more than one person, was obviously mistaken."

James Hicks continued to assert his innocence of the crime for which he had been tried and convicted. The closest alleged statement that the state had been able to provide regarding his supposed guilt was the testimony by Myra and Adrian Cyr in which they said that they had confronted Hicks in Matawaska and accused him of killing their daughter and getting rid of her body. Hicks had replied, "You'll never prove that." The defense argued in its appeal that "this statement is the closest that the State ever gets to a confession or admission, although it is arguably neither."

The defense appealed the case on the basis that the evidence introduced at trial was insufficient to support the jury's finding Hicks guilty of fourth-degree homicide beyond a reasonable standard of proof. It also contended that the jury should have been instructed on fifth-degree homicide and that the statute of limitations had barred a fourth-degree conviction. The state had not proved that Jennie Cyr Hicks was actually dead or that, if she was dead, James Hicks had caused her death. Jennie might still be alive—she might have left the trailer of her own volition or she might have committed suicide. Furthermore, as a final major point of contention, the defense contested that the jury should not have been allowed to hear testimony about Jennie Cyr Hicks's interactions and behavior with her children.[78]

At a November bail hearing, Charles Leadbetter, acting for the state, requested that bail be set at $100,000. Billings requested that bail be set at $10,000 to $15,000. The court set bail at $30,000, with two securities and three conditions. The conditions were that Hicks could not contact any witness, he was required to report in every other Friday and he could not leave the state. The defense subsequently requested reduced bail, arguing that Hicks was not a threat to the community. The state argued that he was.[79]

James Hicks was freed on bail on December 19, 1984. At the time of his release, he stated, "It's beginning to look a lot like Christmas."[80] It seems that for Christmas 1984, James Hicks wanted a new wife. He decided to marry his live-in girlfriend and mother of two of his children, Linda Marquis. The press gave almost as much coverage to this latest twist as it had the murder trial.

James Hicks applied for a marriage license while continuing to assert that he had not murdered Jennie and that she was probably still alive. He could not, however, marry one woman while he was still married to another, which indeed he would have been were Jennie Cyr Hicks still alive. The state had found Hicks guilty of murdering his wife, and thus considered her legally dead, yet no death certificate had been issued for Jennie, as the case was in the appeal process and no body had ever been found. Remarrying while the case was under appeal would be bigamy in the eyes of the law. Hicks did have the option of confessing that he knew Jennie was dead and signing a death certificate, but that he refused to do.

Hicks wrote to the press in late December stating his position. "The State—not me—says she is deceased…The State—not me—should issue the appropriate documents of their convictions or set me free."[81]

Thirty-one-year-old Linda Marquis told a reporter for the *Boston Globe* in January 1985 about the couple's desire to marry. "I can explain it in one word…Love. We'd be married this afternoon if we could."

Hicks stated, "It's hard to explain love. It is just this feeling you have that you think alike…We just want to be married." Marquis said that she would marry Hicks even if he went to jail for murder.[82]

Hicks told the *Boston Globe* that he would not sign Jennie's death certificate. "Well, I didn't admit she was dead in court and I'm certainly not going to do it now." He said that he could not afford to pursue his other legal option: applying for a divorce. To divorce Jennie with his appeal pending, he would have to file for an *in absentia* divorce, as Jennie could not be located to be served with divorce papers. An *in absentia* divorce would cost Hicks hundreds of dollars, if not more—money that he said he simply did not have. He and Linda relied on state welfare to support their six children, then ages three through fourteen. Hicks described himself as a construction worker and automobile mechanic.[83]

The *Globe* article was accompanied by a small headshot of Jennie Hicks, set below a photograph of a smiling James Hicks and Linda Marquis, relaxed for the camera in their Etna house. The *Globe* described Hicks as a "short, blond, bearded man."[84] Certainly, the "short, blond, bearded man" looked pleased to tell his story to the world.

Unfolding events in the case were widely discussed throughout the state and elsewhere. While the legal process continued in 1984, Hicks and Marquis contacted Child Keyppers of Florida, an agency that specialized in searching for missing children and adults. The agency reportedly distributed some twenty thousand posters on Jennie's disappearance.[85]

One Child Keyppers bulletin provided a physical description of Jennie; however, it may not have been favorable to Hicks's arguments for innocence. As well as showing possible surgical scars and a curvature to the spine, it noted a laceration on Jennie's scalp, a scar behind her left ear, fractures of the right clavicle and ribs and an earlier concussion. (Separate reports state that Jennie had been in a car accident a few years earlier, which might explain some of the injuries.) The bulletin stated that Jennie's children had requested that Child Keyppers search for her, in spite of Hicks's conviction for fourth-degree murder. A separate missing persons notice printed by the Maine press provided the same basic description of Jennie but identified her hair as being dark blonde and worn in the style made popular by actress Farrah Fawcett-Majors. (Some of Jennie's friends had called her Farrah because of her hairstyle.)[86]

The press continued to cover the events of 1985. The *Morning Sentinel* reported on the appeal process into the spring and early summer, as did the *Bangor Daily News* and the *Portland Press Herald*. The three papers together essentially blanketed the state with their coverage and distribution. One of the major events they covered in early summer was the Hicks appeal verdict.

The Maine Supreme Court upheld Hicks's conviction on July 9, 1985. The decision was a unanimous one. Justice David A. Nichols wrote the lengthy legal decision. The court rejected all of the appellant's contentions. The court determined that the jury could have concluded, based on the evidence presented at the trial, that James Hicks had knowingly or intentionally killed Jennie Hicks, used her hair to help conceal her injuries, dragged Jennie's body from the trailer and disposed of her body in the many miles of forested land between his home and his place of work in Woodland, Maine. He might have left behind her glasses and purse in his haste.[87]

Hicks and his attorney did not acquiesce. They considered filing an appeal to the United States Supreme Court. Restating many of the points raised in their appeal, J. Hillary Billings told the *Portland Press Herald* that although there had been convictions for homicide without a body in other states, in such cases, or rather in "virtually" every one, there had been a confession. In Hicks's case, there had not even been evidence of a death. In mid-July, Billings was awaiting examination of the court's appeal decision and "considering the appropriateness of an appeal to the U.S. Supreme Court."[88]

James Hicks went back to jail. He turned himself in at the Penobscot County Jail in Bangor and from there was transported to and incarcerated at the Maine State Prison at Thomaston. Even so, James Hicks and Linda Marquis pursued their marital options. A legal void continued to exist for a few weeks after the latest court decision. Hicks and Marquis sought a marriage license immediately after the court ruling but found that there were still a few obstacles. When asked if he would issue a death certificate for Jennie Cyr Hicks, Deputy Attorney General Fernand LaRochelle replied that that would be the job of Chief Medical Examiner Henry F. Ryan. Ryan responded that it was a legal problem and that it was the responsibility of the Maine Office of Vital Records to issue the death certificate. Ryan had never issued a death certificate in the absence of a body, although in some states, coroner's inquests still met to determine a death. Ryan did not have the authority to convene a coroner's inquest. Certification of a death did occur from time to time, however, particularly in instances of fishermen lost at sea. He had not been asked to do the research needed to lead to a possible certification of death in this case.[89]

Michael Fleming of the office of vital records stated that should a controversy arise over the situation, the department would probably seek legal advice from the attorney general's office. The two top officers in his own department were on vacation, so nothing could be done until the following Monday.[90]

That Monday, Linda Marquis received word that she would indeed be receiving a death certificate for Jennie Hicks. This would allow the betrothed couple to secure a marriage license and marry. Marquis told the *Bangor Daily News* that she had contacted the department, had spoken with a secretary in the criminal division and had been informed of the decision. Marquis stated that she hoped she could hold the department at its word. "If not, they'll hear from me again."[91]

Law enforcement had taken Hicks to Thomaston the previous Wednesday, just after the court upheld the jury's verdict. Marquis had not yet been able to visit him, but she hoped to visit him the following week and to marry him in the near future. Marquis said that it did not matter if she had to marry Hicks in prison because she loved him and they had wanted to marry for a long time. Her fiancé, however, was not pleased with the issuing of the death certificate. James, she said, wanted to receive a waiver from the office of vital statistics to allow the marriage, as having a death certificate issued reinforced the claim that Jennie was dead.[92]

In July 1985, Linda Marquis said she believed that her fiancé's former wife was alive and that James Hicks had not harmed her. She said she just knew that Jennie would be found. As she explained it, "You just get good feelings about something, and you know it's going to happen. I feel it is going to happen." She mentioned Child Keyppers and said that more posters of Jennie would be distributed, posters showing a photographic age progression.[93]

So certain was Marquis that Jennie would be found that she said of the court justices, "I'm sure they'll feel a little awkward when Jennie is found, a little embarrassed maybe." She then outlined what she believed to be the failings of the state police and the sheriff's department and suggested that some missing documents might have been deliberately lost.[94]

Marquis told the *Bangor Daily News* that there was one thing she truly wanted: "I want to see him [Hicks] home where he belongs." Likewise, she told the *Morning Sentinel* that "deep down inside I know that he's innocent. I have no doubts whatsoever. We've been waiting to marry for a long time. He's my man."[95]

With the appropriate death certificate issued by the state and filed by James Hicks, Linda Marquis married her man at Thomaston State Prison in August 1985. The wedding ceremony was quiet and brief—the ceremony lasted fifteen minutes and the entire affair, including the cutting and eating of wedding cake, lasted about seventy-five minutes. The couple's six children attended the Friday morning ceremony, as did some members of Hicks's family and a few friends. The couple exchanged their vows in a prison visiting room and were married by a Pentecostal minister from Carmel. After the ceremony, the new Mrs. Hicks and the children were able to visit with James Hicks for a couple of hours and then returned home. The bride told the *Sentinel* that she and her husband felt more secure about the children, as she was now the legal mother of the two children to whom Jennie Hicks had given birth. To date, Hicks had served sixteen months of his ten-year sentence. As for the remainder of his term, she said, "He's worth waiting for."[96]

While she waited, Linda Hicks sought new legal representation for her husband. Billings had quit the case. By mid-August, he had decided not to pursue a U.S. Supreme Court appeal. He had prepared a brief for the Supreme Court, and another lawyer could make use of it. Hicks had until early September to file an appeal, and that deadline could be extended. Billings said that he wished Hicks "the best of luck."[97]

Linda Hicks told the *Bangor Daily News* on August 23, the night of her marriage, that she was looking for someone "who knows his way around federal courts, who does not charge a lot of money, and who practices in Bangor" to represent her husband. She had consulted a few attorneys already, but their responses had not been encouraging. "They say the case is 'too time consuming,' 'there's not enough money,' and they've got to 'look after their other clients.'…A poor person just can't get a lawyer." Linda Hicks vowed to keep searching. She reiterated that during the seven years she had lived with James Hicks, he had never acted violently toward her—proof, she thought, that he was simply not a killer.[98]

But he was.

CHAPTER FOUR

FREE TO ROAM, FREE TO KILL

James Hicks Walks Again

As the years passed, the marriage of James and Linda Marquis Hicks ran into serious trouble. And although Hicks was in jail, law enforcement and those who loved Jerilyn Towers did not give up on her case. Her disappearance from the Gateway Lounge in 1982 had not been forgotten. Law enforcement had come to believe that James Rodney Hicks was indeed responsible for her death. Prosecutors had not had enough evidence to indict Hicks in the early 1980s, but they had been able to put together a case against him for the murder of his wife, Jennie Lynn Cyr. While Hicks served his time at the Thomaston State Prison for that murder, police pondered the Jerilyn Towers case. As the time for Hicks's release came closer, law enforcement concerns and activities escalated and continued for the next several years.

The Maine State Police had in the interim, however, been forced to temporarily close the file on Jerilyn Towers. In October 1986, while Hicks remained incarcerated, Maine State Police detective Richard Reitchell submitted a recommendation that the file be closed. Reitchell wrote that "although this case appears to be a homicide, the body of Jerilyn Towers has not been located." The investigation's results "would lead one to believe that James Hicks…is most certainly responsible for Jerilyn Towers' death." But due to the lack of new leads, he requested that the case "be closed to our files pending new information."[99] Yet the investigation did continue for the Newport Police Department, if not the Maine State Police.

James Hicks served six years, five months and fourteen days in prison for the murder of Jennie Lynn Cyr Hicks. Released in 1990, he was called a "model prisoner" by officials. When queried about this characterization of Hicks, Deputy Attorney General William Stokes stated in 2009, "He probably was. Many of them are model prisoners…Their problem is with women." Apparently, the incarcerated men did not necessarily have problems comporting themselves reasonably well in a prison setting.[100] Unfortunately, Hicks's problems with women continued after his release.

Hicks's marriage to the former Linda Marquis collapsed while he was in prison. Always a man to overlap relationships, Hicks had already started seeing another woman, Karen Gomm. The two were married while Hicks was in prison and divorced in 1991 or 1992. Karen had met James Hicks through her sister, Melinda Hicks, who was married to James Hicks's brother Steve. James was in a pre-release program in Bangor, and he and Karen started their relationship through correspondence.[101]

Karen had two young children when she began her relationship with Hicks. The Maine Department of Human Services subsequently removed the children from her custody, an action that she blamed on James Hicks. The children went to live with their father. Karen and James's marriage had numerous problems, and at times when the couple fought, he would say to her, "I'm not going to tell you if I did kill Jennie, but I'm not going to tell you I didn't either." James Hicks would then laugh. There was an element of violence in the marriage, and Hicks perhaps wanted his wife to be afraid of him and what he might be capable of doing to her. The couple separated three times before finally divorcing.[102]

James Rodney Hicks again took up with one woman while still deeply involved with another. He started a lengthy affair in late 1990 with Louise Robertson. The two met at the Brewer Twin City Motel, where both worked, a place that, like the Gateway Lounge, would prove significant in Hicks's life—and not just his love life. Louise knew that Hicks was married to Karen at the time. She said that she was suspicious of some of the things Hicks did but that he was never physically abusive to her. She said he did have "an enormous sexual appetite" and that at the end of the relationship he started getting rough with her. She lived in a mobile home park in Bangor with him for a while. They broke up a few times and then separated for good after he began seeing yet another woman, Lynn Willette, who was also an employee of the motel. Robertson had a child with Hicks, a daughter named Georgia,[*] in 1992. Hicks did not acknowledge that the child was his until he was forced to take a blood test, which came up positive for his paternity.[103]

Robertson's relationship with Hicks lasted about four years, from roughly 1990 to 1994. It was on-and-off affair. As for what had happened to Jennie Cyr, Hicks told Robertson, "That is between me and God." He did tell her that he had had another daughter in Bangor who had been molested and murdered. He showed her a photograph of some girls in a Bangor school, and the girl in question would have been born between 1983 and 1984 and died in 1989 or 1990. Robertson also stated that Hicks was a "petty thief"—he was always stealing supplies and items from vending machines—and that he became "paranoid at the sight of blood."[104]

Police interviewed Robertson and Karen Gomm Hicks in the 1990s because they were continuing their investigation of James Hicks. Linda Marquis Hicks was present at one of the police interviews with Karen Hicks. She was also present at one of the interviews with Louise Robertson. She was present because she had become afraid of her ex-husband and had developed relationships with some of the other women in his life. Linda Hicks had finally come to believe that James Hicks was indeed a murderer.[105]

James Ricker of Newport had continued to conduct interviews and had undertaken numerous "land searches" over the previous decade, ever since Jerilyn Towers disappeared. He had received several calls concerning possible grave sites and had investigated them. He rode on horseback over the area, including the Hicks property in Etna. Some leads seemed reliable; others, less so. In one instance, a psychic contacted him and said that she could see Jerilyn Towers clearly and that Jerilyn was not wearing shoes. Ricker looked in the spot she indicated, but to no avail. When Ricker was later asked if James Hicks had taken issue with Ricker searching his land, Ricker said, "Hey…It wasn't posted. No one asked me to leave. I was looking for worms."[106] There was, at times, an element of comedy or grand farce in Hicks's interactions with law enforcement in the 1980s and 1990s. Hicks was often forced to go along with reports and activities that he hated or else risk making himself look even more guilty.

People other than law enforcement also checked out the Hicks property over the years. Tammy Price, Jerilyn's daughter, drove out to the Hicks property by herself one night, just to look around. She felt that her mother was there. She said in 2009, "I went to pull into his driveway, and slipped off into the ditch." She panicked, thinking that Hicks had come to the door—someone had. It may indeed have been James Hicks, as it was during the early 1990s and Hicks was out of prison. Tammy was able to get her car out of the ditch and drive off before anything further occurred. This was not her only visit to the property.[107]

At about the same time that Tammy Price was investigating the Hicks property, James Ricker interviewed Linda Marquis Hicks after learning of her divorce from James Hicks. The 1991 meeting took place in Ricker's police office. According to Ricker's report:

> *Linda had come to my office to set the record straight for any problems we may have had during the first investigation. I initiated the conversation by asking Linda if she could give me some type of personality profile of James*

Hicks. She stated that he was very possessive, extremely jealous, and had a severe temper. She stated she was never allowed to wear makeup or go outside the home unless she was with him. The only place she was allowed to go was to ceramics class.[108]

Marquis further stated that she had previously lied to the police. James Hicks had told her to tell the authorities that on the night that Towers disappeared, he had arrived home at 1:00 a.m. However, she now stated, he had actually returned home at 4:00 a.m. He had told her to say this before he was convicted of homicide in the death of his wife, during the trial and after his conviction. She said that she had lied in order to protect Hicks.[109]

Marquis also told Ricker that the car James Hicks had been driving that October night in 1982 was still located in the backyard of the Hicks property. She said that Hicks had removed the entire interior of the car, including its carpet and headliner. According to Marquis, the car had been, as far as she knew, "still running when he drove it to the rear of their property and stripped it."[110]

In autumn 1994, Linda Marquis Hicks granted permission to James Ricker, now police chief in Newport, to remove the 1973 Plymouth from the property in Etna. She turned over the blue four-door car to Ricker, as she was convinced that Jimmy had stripped it because it contained evidence. Ricker conferred with a laboratory specialist, who stated that the crime lab would not be able to obtain evidence from the car so many years after the alleged incident. Ricker asked Marquis to contact him should she remember anything further.[111]

Before Linda offered up the car for investigation, Vance Tibbetts and Jean Worthley, brother and sister of Jerilyn Towers, had contacted the Newport Police Department. They did so in February 1994. Vance Tibbetts stated that while serving time as a convicted felon in the Maine State Prison, he had met with fellow inmate James Hicks to try to determine whether Hicks had killed his sister. The warden and assistant warden were, according to Tibbetts, present at the meeting. Tibbetts said that, among other questions, he had specifically asked Hicks if he had killed Jerilyn. Hicks, Tibbetts alleged, told him that Jerilyn had left the Gateway Lounge that night with a truck driver. Hicks refused to answer any further questions or to submit to a lie detector exam. He then asked to leave the room. The siblings reviewed some of Ricker's records while at the police station and told Ricker that they "wanted to try and end this and bury their sister."[112]

Subsequent records state that Tibbetts had contacted the deputy warden requesting the meeting with Hicks. His request was granted, and prison staff escorted Tibbetts to the segregated area. Hicks acted extremely nervous, "even with all the prison personnel and prison guards present…He wouldn't look Vance Tibbetts in the eye." In response to Tibbetts's question about what had happened to his sister, "Hicks responded that Jerilyn had left the Gateway with a truck driver." When Tibbetts asked if Hicks was willing to take a lie detector test, Hicks said that he would need to consult with his attorney. Handwritten on the report was the statement, "Vance repeatedly asked Hicks to look him in the eye and deny he had anything to do with Jerilyn's disappearance. Hicks never looked Vance Tibbetts in the eye once."[113]

While Chief Ricker pursued other possible connections between Hicks and Towers, Jeri's sister and brother contacted Jennie's mother and, through her, obtained a telephone number for Linda Marquis Hicks. Members of the two families talked about Hicks. He had already left his then current wife, Karen Hicks, who lived nearby in Hampden. Tibbetts then purportedly contacted Karen Hicks.[114]

During the same time period, Linda Hicks informed police that James Hicks had contacted her by telephone and allegedly told her, "That missing girl in Newport. Her brother called Karen and was asking all kinds of questions; they are just trying to put me back in jail." The two of them then talked about what time Hicks had gotten home that night in 1982. Hicks insisted that she knew he had been home at about 1:00 a.m. She told him that she knew it had been 4:00 a.m. She told Ricker she was afraid that Jimmy might do something to hurt her because of the conflict.[115] Yet, in 1982 Hicks had once stated that he had awoken in a campground at 3:50 a.m. on the morning of Jerilyn's disappearance. He had already incriminated himself.

Linda Hicks requested that Ricker set up a meeting with Jean Worthley, Vance Tibbetts and one of Hicks's friends. The meeting took place on March 8, 1994, and included a member of the state crime laboratory. As a result of the meeting, Ricker reported that he had made several searches for bodies in the area and now believed that he might have been looking in the wrong place. Ricker also identified several people who needed to be interviewed or re-interviewed regarding the Towers case and raised the possibility that there might be other related missing persons cases.[116]

Other factors in the investigation of James Hicks had surfaced over the years and would continue to do so in the following years. One of the women involved with Hicks told police officers that he had sexually abused her. She said that he was very sexually aggressive and had to have sex at least once a day, sometimes two or three times. He would slap her and become enraged if she fought back. She said he liked to tie her to the bed with pantyhose or clothesline and sometimes penetrated her with foreign objects. Other women related similar sexual practices. With some of his partners, Hicks

James Ricker, nemesis of James Hicks. Ricker investigated the disappearance of Jerilyn Towers for almost twenty years and was involved in other disappearances associated with Hicks. Ricker is shown here in his Newport town office, where he now serves as the town manager. *Photograph by Trudy Irene Scee.*

was perhaps more demanding than he was abusive. One woman said that he liked to have sex on back roads, and she and another woman said that he especially liked sex at a gravel pit. Over the course of three decades, a surprising number of women made statements about Hicks.[117]

Of the many children who had lived with Hicks or encountered him through family relationships, a few of them had been, or their parents said they had been, abused by James Hicks. The alleged abuse happened when the children were young. (Police also had some evidence that Hicks may have been physically and sexually abused as a child.) Accusations of Hicks killing or injuring animals also surfaced, along with numerous accusations of Hicks intimidating witnesses or potential witnesses, directly or through other individuals. Hicks may not have been formally charged with such crimes because of insufficient evidence and existing statutes of limitations.[118] Furthermore, by the mid- to late 1990s, when much of this information came to light, police were trying to build another case against Hicks, one that would keep him in jail for the rest of his life.

By the late 1990s, two more events of major consequence had happened. James Hicks had married another woman, and another woman had gone missing.

CHAPTER FIVE

LIGHTNING STRIKES THRICE

The Case of Lynn Ann Willette

In 1994, thirty-nine-year-old Lynn Ann Willette applied for a job at the Twin City Motel in Brewer, Maine. The motel was located just across the Penobscot River from Bangor, a few miles out on outer Wilson Street. James Hicks, the motel's maintenance supervisor, interviewed Willette and hired her to work with him. Hicks was involved with Louise Robertson at the time, but, as had happened before in his past, he cavalierly started up one relationship while actively involved in another.

Lynn Willette had lived outside of Maine a few times in her life, a new characteristic among the women with whom Hicks became seriously involved. Lynn was born on August 29, 1955, in Bangor to Jane and Vincent Hinks. She liked to travel and was sometimes described as a "free spirit." She graduated from Brewer High School in 1972, married and divorced four times, served in the United States Army and had some paramedical experience.[119]

Lynn, sometimes known as Lynnie, had brown hair in the mid-1990s, often tinted to a reddish brown or auburn shade and worn at about shoulder length, sometimes a bit longer or shorter. She was a fairly slender woman, who generally wore, quite literally, rose-tinted glasses. Her ears were pierced, and in addition to earrings, she often wore rings, in particular a gold wedding band and a silver ring with a gold-green stone. She had a few tattoos. Lynn's mother and sister lived nearby in Orrington, just south of Brewer. Her father was hospitalized at the Veterans' Hospital in Bangor.[120]

Hicks soon moved into Lynn's apartment on South Main Street in Brewer. Louise Robertson ended her relationship with Hicks at about this time, and Hicks needed a place to live. Hicks and Willette continued to work together at the Twin City Motel throughout 1995. They had a pit bull dog named Felon and often other animals as well.[121]

The apartment that the two shared was located behind two others in a two-story house. It faced the Penobscot River, with a few hundred yards of business/industrial property in between. The other side of the building fronted busy South Main Street. The building was close to I-395, a highway bypass route connecting to I-95. The apartment had a small living room, kitchen and bedroom, a bathroom and access to the basement. Two people lived in one of the other apartments and three people shared the third.[122]

According to Hicks and others, although Lynn and Hicks moved in together, they rarely had sex. This may have been due to a health issue, or perhaps Lynn was using her health as an excuse not to have sex with Hicks with any great frequency. Hicks did admit that Lynn would tell him when they could have sex. A woman determining when he might have sex with her was seemingly a new phenomenon in Hicks's life.[123]

In 1995 and early 1996, Lynn was taking classes at Beal College, a small Bangor school that offered degrees in business, medical studies and law enforcement. Her courses included English, medical terminology, math and typewriting. Surviving papers show Lynn to have been an intelligent

Lynn Willette, shown here in the early 1980s, would come to regret her association with James Hicks. *Photograph courtesy of a friend of Willette.*

woman—one who loved people and animals yet was having trouble in her relations with both. Of greatest concern were her relationships with men and dogs. Lynn had had a romantic relationship in North Carolina that had ended badly and a dog she loved very much that had died. She seemed to have tried unsuccessfully to replace both. Whatever her problems in her relationship with Hicks, she was, at least at times, turning her angst inward against herself, questioning almost everything about herself, even her ability to care for her current dogs. Yet everyone who related stories about Lynn spoke of her great love for her dogs.

A practice paper indicated her struggles in early 1996. As she had her own typewriter, she may have written this and others at her apartment. One assignment seems to overlap another, yet it was overall a happier day of work than some others. For example, in one place, under the caption "what I like to do with my spare time," she spoke of her favorite television shows and wrote, "I also like to spend time laughing with my two dogs. I like to watch them play together. [T]hey get real excited sometimes and I have to holler at them to calm down." She wrote that she went to her mother's house to spend time with her during the weekends and watched the NASCAR races on Sundays.[124]

Lynn wove a second practice assignment in between the lines of the first. She wrote that her weekends were "always the same." On Saturday mornings, she wrote, "I get up and study my math and English, that usually lasts about three or four hours. I then do the housework. I vacuum the floors, dust, and do the washing."[125]

A third practice paper titled "My Life" shows a more depressed Lynn. This time she wrote in all capital letters:

> *My life is so hard to explain...Ever since I left N.C. I just seem to be drifting...I want someone to share my life and then I don't. I want to be in love, but I can't get over the feeling that I had for G——...I need to be alone to make decisions that will make me a better person...I have been trying to replace Kala, with many dogs...Will I feel guilty if I get rid of Felon. Will I get rid of Lacey.[126]*

Lynn continued to question whether she should keep her dogs or give them away, wondering if they were happy with her in her current situation. She questioned herself, "WHAT DO I WANT. WHAT DO I WANT. WHAT DO I WANT." In something of an answer she wrote, "I WANT KALA BACK. I WANT TO GO BACK TO 1985. AND DO IT AGAIN. I JUST WANT TO STOP EVERYTHING." She wrote that she was always on edge and was tired of hiding in the bathroom to cry. She questioned how she was able to keep going and why other people did not notice her distress. She also wrote that she was tired of being overweight, although there is no evidence that she was ever appreciably overweight.[127]

A narration assignment for Lynn's English class provides further insight and explanation. In the 1995 college assignment titled "Kala," Lynn wrote:

> *A part of my heart was lost when my dog died. We had only been together less than three years, when that fateful day came. The friendship started when I went to look at a litter of black lab Puppies. As I was trying to decide which one of the girls I wanted, I had a shadow following me. She wasn't my first choice, but it was obvious that I was hers...Finally, I decided to give the fuzzy, black puppy a second look. When I looked into her eyes, I knew I had found my best friend. The next couple of years, we were inseparable. She helped me through a very painful relationship, and a hard breakup. I always felt safe when we were together.*

Lynn went on to write that after working for ten hours one day she went out in the yard with Kala to relax. She decided to walk across the street to buy some French fries. Kala had never followed her across the road before, so she thought it was safe to leave Kala in the yard. But, she wrote:

> *That day she decided to follow me. The next moments in time went in slow motion. I saw the car come along and hit her. I saw her fly through the air and land at least a hundred feet away. She got up and came toward me, and collapsed at my feet. I sat on the edge of the road, holding her for forty-five minutes as she died...After three years, I still have a tear for Kala when I think of her.*[128]

When Kala died, James Hicks had not yet moved in with Lynn. After Hicks moved in, Lynn wrote of all the mistakes she had made, of her guilt over what had happened to Kala and of her mistaken relationships. Kala was not there to make her feel safe in 1996, a time when Lynn most needed to be safe.

Lynn wrote another essay, titled "What I Want in Life," at about the same time. This may have been the paper that she was drafting in her typing practice. She stated that she had not been happy since she came back from North Carolina and that she had once made the mistake of trying to reunite with her boyfriend there. She wrote that her life had "been going downhill since Kala died." After repeating other statements from her typing practice, she wrote that she wanted to be alone and "be independent so I can make decisions on what I really want, and not be made to make decisions because I have no other choice." Lynn wrote of her dogs, of missing Kala, of wondering if she should give her current ones away. "I don't know if getting another lab will make me happy," she wrote. She ended her essay with more concerns about her dogs.[129]

A person with whose family Lynn had lived a few years earlier confirmed that both Kala and Lynn were unique. Lynn had stayed with the family before she met Hicks, when she was back in Maine but working at a store in Brewer. Kala had lived at the house with her and became attached in her own way to the family. One day, Kala perhaps saved a young child. As the father of the young boy, who was little more than a toddler at the time, described it:

> *There was a bunch of us having a cookout. Michael was just a baby, about two years old, and Kala took him for a walk. I don't know how else to describe it. He was with us all, and then he wasn't. There were eight adults there…and none of us saw it happen. Then we realized it and we all ran. I yelled and told everyone where to go, and we all took off.*[130]

Everyone went in a different direction. "I just happened to take the right side. I was in a panic," he said. He ran around the side of the block where the house was, headed down the next block and turned the corner. Then he saw them, the boy and the dog, headed his way.

> *I called them both. They were on the sidewalk, walking toward me, and she would just give him a nudge with her head to keep him away from the road. She was on the outside of the sidewalk, the road side, and she would just nudge him a little to make sure he stayed on the sidewalk. I caught up with them in no time. I was just squeezing him, and loving the dog. She acted like she was just doing her job. No big deal.*[131]

Years after the incident, after Kala had died and Lynn had disappeared, the father would remember the event with both admiration and fear. He was an overprotective father by most standards, and one could hear his panic in the retelling.

Reminiscing further about Lynnie, the child's father said, "She loved her wine, but she was an interesting person. She was cool." He also recalled that "she always seemed to have one dog who I think she loved more than she loved people…She never went anywhere without her dog."[132]

Felon, however, was one dog who went places without Lynn. The pit bull frequently escaped—or was let out—from the apartment that Lynn shared with Hicks. Felon, despite his name, never really got into any trouble. But, as Sargent Jay Munson of the Brewer Police Department later described the situation, "Felon would always get loose, and I'd stop and pick him up. He'd get in the car and ride around with me for a while." Munson got tired of taking Felon to the dog pound, so he would call Lynn and let her know that he had the dog. "She was always the one who came and picked him up," Munson said, although once or twice he had taken the dog home. On one of these occasions, Hicks came to the door and took the dog inside but said little to the officer, who was new to the department and was serving patrol duty. Munson said that Lynn seemed to him to be "a person who worked hard, who had to work hard for everything she had, who loved her dog." He said that she also seemed rather jovial and polite.[133] It seems peculiar that Lynn would allow Felon to get loose after what had happened to Kala, but of course, there were two people living at the apartment.

Eventually, Lynn did decide to leave Hicks and to keep her dogs. She had recently acquired another black Labrador, a female she named Nikki.

Lynn Willette moved into an apartment on South Main Street in Brewer in the 1990s. She was joined there by James Hicks and, it seemed, disappeared from the apartment, whose entrance was on the south side of the building. *Photograph by Trudy Irene Scee.*

She had signed up for more college classes after she had written her essay "Kala," but her enrollment lapsed in the spring of 1996, perhaps due to her relationship with Hicks. Hicks could be extremely possessive, and that possessiveness may have played a role in her decision to leave Hicks.

By autumn 1995, James Hicks believed that he was being stalked by Vance Tibbetts, Jerilyn Towers's brother. Hicks called the Brewer Police Department in late August 1995 and made a complaint against Tibbetts. Hicks told Sergeant Mike Hall that Tibbetts had just gotten out of jail and was following him around. Hall contacted Tibbetts, who said that Hicks was suspected of having killed his sister and that he just wanted some photographs of Hicks. He did not say why he wanted them. He advised the Brewer Police Department that if it should ever have a missing persons complaint, Hicks would be a good suspect.[134]

The Brewer police then contacted Detective Joseph W. Zamboni of the Maine State Police and asked him about Hicks. As part of the agency entrusted with murders throughout the state and other serious crimes, Zamboni would be in a position to delve into the situation. Zamboni later said of the telephone call, "I got a call from the Brewer PD. They said that Hicks was complaining about Vance Tibbetts. I didn't know who Jimmy Hicks was at the time, but Hicks said Vance was stalking him, that he thought Hicks had killed his sister."

"So," Zamboni continued, "I went to see Vance. He said that he would hound Hicks until the day he died. I told Hicks, 'This is not someone to mess with. He will kill you.' I asked him to take a polygraph."[135]

Zamboni said in 2009 that he could not take a confrontational approach with Hicks. He knew that Hicks would shut down if he did. So Zamboni decided to take more of a "we're partners in this" approach when dealing with Hicks, while Ricker, he said, was more confrontational.[136] Hicks's mind was essentially the only crime scene they had, and Zamboni wanted to keep communications open.

In early February 1996, Detective Zamboni conducted an interview with Hicks at the Twin City Motel. The topic of the interview was again the possibility of Hicks's taking a lie detector test. Hicks told Zamboni that he had talked it over with his mother, who was then in the hospital, and with his girlfriend, Lynn Willette. According to Hicks, Lynn had told him that "he didn't have to prove anything to anybody." He said he did want to take the test, but not right away, perhaps sometime that summer.[137]

Lynn Willette came into the room during the interview. Zamboni talked to her briefly about the polygraph, and she then looked at Hicks and told him, "You're a big boy. It's up to you." Zamboni told Hicks that he would check in with him later and left the premises.[138]

Lynn Willette worked at the Brewer Twin City Motel with James Hicks until she disappeared in 1996. Other female friends or partners of James Hicks also worked there with him during the 1990s. The motel has since changed ownership and has been remodeled and renamed. *Photograph by Trudy Irene Scee.*

The space where Joe Zamboni interviewed Hicks was a back building at the motel, sometimes called the annex. It was an addition built to hold some of the nicer guest rooms, as well as a banquet center. However, the plans for the annex did not work out as anticipated. In the mid-1990s, Hicks made it into his private domain, especially the downstairs section, where he had a paint and repair shop. He used the area as a maintenance facility. Hicks had mirrors set up so that he could monitor the entire hallway leading to the space that he used for his office.[139]

Zamboni interviewed Hicks on other occasions during 1995 and early 1996. Lynn was present at Hicks's request. Hicks said that he wanted her there as a witness because he did not trust the police. (James Ricker would later say that Hicks always liked to have "some woman around to stick up for him.") Hicks told Zamboni at least once that he loved Lynn Willette and that she was the best thing that had ever happened to him. Zamboni later stated that he thought that Lynn started backing away from Hicks in part due to the ongoing Towers investigation.[140] Hicks was caught in the middle, wanting to proclaim his innocence and tell Zamboni to go away but also feeling that he had to cooperate to show his innocence. There was no real evidence against him, but there was none in favor of him either.

Lynn, unhappy in her relationship with Hicks, began to tell friends that he was too possessive. She said that she "needed more space." The couple decided to break up, or, at least, Lynn decided that she was going to break up with him. Lynn decided that if he wouldn't leave, she would, even though the apartment had originally been hers. They had lived together for about a year and a half. At least initially, it seemed that the breakup was amicable.[141]

Willette began moving her belongings to her mother's house in Orrington. She took her dog Nikki there after building her a safe enclosure and stayed with her mother while continuing to move out of the apartment. She had her own car, a blue 1988 Toyota Tercel. James Hicks drove a red Chevy Blazer at the time.[142]

On Sunday, May 26, 1996, James Hicks called the Brewer Police Department and reported Lynn Willette missing. He told Sergeant Mike Hall that Lynn had failed to show up for a family cookout that day and had not been seen since Saturday.[143] Another woman had gone missing.

Hicks told police that, although they had split up, he and Lynn had left the motel together at about 12:00 p.m. the previous day and had gone to the apartment on South Main Street. He said that they had had sexual relations, spent the afternoon together and had eaten sandwiches from the nearby Big Apple Store. They had then gone shopping and for a long drive in the country. That night, after the drive, he had let Lynn off at their apartment, and she had gotten into her car and driven away. Lynn never made it to her mother's house that night. Hicks insisted that he did not know what had happened to her and that he had not done anything to harm her.[144]

Hicks told investigators that Lynn had been depressed and insinuated more than once that she might have been suicidal.[145] Her writings thus became part of the case. Although Lynn's writings do indicate that she might have been despondent over the previous months, her decision to move away from Hicks and to keep her dogs may well have indicated that she was resolving some of the major issues in her life.

Hicks described forty-year-old Lynn's tattoos and other distinguishing marks soon after she disappeared. He said that she had " a [green] heart on her right shoulder and a green colored chain going down the front of her chest and shoulder." She also had "a thistle on her left wrist above her hand, and a green and pink flower." She had a birthmark on her left hip.[146] It later became apparent that Hicks had good reason beyond his intimate relationship with Lynn to know all about her tattoos.

Two neighbors interviewed in the days following Lynn's disappearance testified that they had seen Hicks exit his red Blazer and enter the apartment alone on May 25, shortly after he had punched out of work. They did not see

Lynn Willette arrive. The homeowner, Dagmar Lee, also saw Hicks's vehicle between noon and one o'clock. Dagmar had had to make a telephone call and asked Hicks if she could use his phone. He said that she could, but as she entered the apartment, he closed the door to the bedroom and said that she had interrupted him and Lynn about to have sex. She said that he said something, as though to Lynn, but that she did not hear Lynn answer. Lee considered herself one of Lynn's friends and found the whole incident peculiar.[147] No witnesses surfaced in the days and months following Lynn's disappearance who could corroborate James Hicks's statements.

The Maine State Police and Brewer Police Department tried to retrace Hicks's steps on the day that Lynn disappeared. The Big Apple Store, where Hicks said that he had bought sandwiches for himself and Lynn, did not have a corresponding receipt for that date and time. Hicks claimed that the two had stopped at various stores during their drive, yet no one remembered seeing him or her. Not one person remembered seeing the two together at any time since they had supposedly left work together that Saturday.

Zamboni visited the South Main Street apartment and saw what appeared to be a spot of blood on the carpet. When he returned a few days later, the stain was gone. Hicks admitted that Lynn's blood had been in the living room. He said that one of the dogs had run into a door and pushed it into Lynn's face, and the incident had given her a bloody nose.[148]

Perhaps to take the pressure off, Hicks told police that he had seen Lynn on May 24, the day before she disappeared, riding around in a Saab convertible with her sister, Wendy, and a man. He said that Lynn had been in front with the driver, her sister in the backseat, and that he had argued with Lynn about it on May 25. He knew where the guy lived. When questioned, Wendy said that they indeed had been with a man that day. She had asked Lynn to have a drink with her and a high school friend that Friday afternoon. The friend lived in Brewer and worked as a car salesman in Skowhegan. Hicks later indicated that he had thought that Lynn was lying to him about the man. He thought she may have been involved with him.[149]

Police searched the Bangor-Brewer area extensively in the days after Lynn vanished for any sign of her or her vehicle. In light of Hicks's past, they suspected foul play and tried to determine how Hicks might have killed her and hidden the evidence. They were especially curious about how he could have hidden Lynn's Tercel somewhere and returned undetected to Brewer. They searched back roads and gravel pits for signs of Lynn or her car and even conducted an air search.

On Friday, May 31, Lynn's car was found, locked and parked in the back row of Dysart's Truck Stop in Hermon, just off I-95 and Route 2. When

Zamboni told Hicks that police had recovered Lynn's car, Hicks asked what was in it. Zamboni said that there was nothing in it. Hicks said that that was not true—he claimed that there had been several things in it, including some tools, receipts, a dog collar and leash and fast-food trash. Police had already established that when Hicks and Willette had gone anywhere together, they always traveled in his Blazer, never in her Tercel. If they were apart, Lynn always drove her car and Hicks, his SUV.[150]

The detective later stated that the fact that Hicks, who never drove Lynn's car or rode in it, had been able to "rattle off about twelve things" that had been in the car, some of the items not in plain sight, was significant. "He was either subconsciously or intentionally giving stuff away." The detective worked with the media that year, and every time there was something in the news, Hicks would get rattled. When the car was found, Zamboni had banged on Hicks's door at about 1:00 a.m. and said to Hicks, "Good news Jimmy. We found the car." Zamboni continued to use the "we're partners together in this, let's figure out what happened to Lynn" approach with Hicks over the following months.[151]

After the police located Lynn's vehicle, Hicks reportedly stated that she had run off with a trucker. Hicks's mythical truck driver was back. And, as with Jennie Cyr's and Lynn Towers's families, Lynn's family insisted that she would not have left without calling to let them know where she was going. No calls came in. Furthermore, Lynn's bank account was not used, nor was her paycheck cashed after she disappeared. Lynn had also not made any financial arrangements for her car loan.[152]

On June 3, Zamboni interviewed Dennis Wallace of Auto Credit of Bangor. Lynn had financed her car with the company for almost eighteen months. During that time, Lynn had come in every week to make a car payment. She had not been in since she disappeared. Wallace described Lynn as "always friendly, upbeat, and talkative. She usually had her dogs with her." He had had no idea that she might be leaving.[153]

Also in early June, Zamboni interviewed Teena Adams, owner of Riverside Resale located just across the street from Lynn's former apartment. Adams told the detective that she had sold a VCR and a boombox to Lynn and that she had bought a pit bull from Hicks and Willette. And, she added, "two birds came with it, apparently because they liked the dog." The dog was likely Felon. A member of the Brewer Police Department later said, "My understanding is that he [Hicks] did not like the pit bull, and that may have been why they got rid of it." Hicks had, since the transaction, called the store and said that he wanted the birds back, or some payment for them. He had also come into the store to see an employee and slammed his fist on the counter when he did not get the results he sought.[154]

Hicks called Lynn's sister to ask her if she was going to keep Nikki because he wanted the dog for himself. He also allegedly told Wendy that if Lynn had gone off with a trucker, she would probably return in a month or so. He called again a few days later and talked about a man with whom Lynn had had a relationship in North Carolina. Hicks claimed that this man had beaten her, yet "she thought the world of this guy." Wendy suspected that Hicks had been going through her sister's papers.[155] Although Lynn's own words support the claim that she had cared greatly for a man in North Carolina, no evidence exists that he beat her.

Lynn's dogs became the prime subject of another interview. Speaking with Joseph Zamboni and Dave Clewley of the Brewer Police Department, Hicks stated that Lynn would get very depressed about every four months and "sell the dog or something." He said that Lynn did not like living in Maine but that she had treated him well, and he had trusted her more than he had trusted any other woman. He said that they used to walk the dogs together often, the most recent dogs being Lacey and Nikki. He thought that the dog Lynn had really liked was Nikki but that maybe she had not taken Nikki with her "because of Kala." He said that he still had Lacey, but Nikki was at Lynn's mother's house. He said that Lacey missed Lynn and kept looking for her. He also said that Lynn had dropped out of her medical studies. Lynn's sister subsequently told police that perhaps only one of the two dogs was really hers, the one at their mother's, and that there was no way she would have left the area without taking Nikki with her.[156]

In addition to the issues surrounding the dogs, Hicks said that Lynn was a picky eater—she would not eat lettuce or tomatoes—and that he thought she was bulimic, misused laxatives and had other eating disorders. He stressed her depression again and suggested that she had more serious mental health issues.[157] Unfortunately, rumors about whether Lynn ate lettuce or tomatoes, or whether she purged or abused laxatives, did not help police locate her. Police believed that James Rodney Hicks had killed Lynn Willette—and not because of her dietary habits.

Police interviewed a few members of Hicks's family in 1996, people who generally did not think Hicks had killed Jennie or Lynn. One family member, however, told them that he did not think Hicks would ever go back to jail, no matter what.[158] By this time, key law enforcement personnel firmly believed that Hicks had killed Lynn. The problem was, as always, proving it.

Lynn's mother, Jane Hincks, had also come to believe that Lynn was dead. According to Lynn's sister, when she told her mother of Hicks's past, her mother had cried and then said, "She was my baby you know. She's gone. I'm her mother and I can feel it."[159]

Lightning Strikes Thrice

During the months that followed, Brewer and Maine State Police detectives participated in a series of operations to try to determine exactly what had happened to Lynn Willette. They placed surveillance on James Hicks but obtained no immediately usable evidence against him. They decided to take Hicks on a long drive so that he could show them just where he and Lynn had supposedly gone on the day she disappeared. They wanted to give Hicks an opportunity to talk—an opportunity to slip up or to say too much. They asked him to run through exactly what had happened on that last day. He said that after they clocked out, there had been a problem with a circuit breaker in one of the rooms in the motel annex. This gave Zamboni an important clue, one that led him to believe that Hicks had killed Lynn at the motel.[160] Yet there was still not enough evidence to convict Hicks of a crime.

While Joseph Zamboni continued to investigate Lynn's disappearance, including assembling a National Crime Information Center (NCIC) missing persons packet for her, he also, along with Chief James Ricker of Newport, continued to look into the disappearance of Jerilyn Towers. The two men kept in contact with each other over the months that followed. Linda Marquis went under hypnosis in 1997. She divulged certain facts and possible locations of interest regarding the Towers case while under hypnosis, but none proved immediately fruitful. Zamboni and Ricker together interviewed Karen Hicks and Louise Robertson to try to uncover any information or behavioral patterns that might help them uncover what Hicks had done to the missing women.[161]

Despite his proclaimed love for Lynn, James Hicks did not wait celibately for her return. He found another woman, one with whom he quickly moved in, within a few months of Lynn's disappearance. His old patterns were holding.

CHAPTER SIX

HELL MOVES ON

James Hicks and His Bride Go West

By late September 1996, only four months after his girlfriend and supposed great love had vanished, James Hicks had moved in with an eighteen-year-old girl, Brandie Mayo of Levelland, Texas. By November, they were reportedly arguing, and Hicks refused to let her leave the relationship.[162]

Maine State Police detective Joseph Zamboni contacted Brandie's mother, Ann Mayo, to apprise her of the situation and of Hicks's background. She told him that Brandie had met Hicks while working part time at the Twin City Motel as a chambermaid, but her daughter was also a personal care attendant (PCA). She said that her daughter was a good kid but suffered from some self-esteem issues and was concerned about her weight. She thought that James Hicks was brainwashing her child.

Ann Mayo had seen bruises on her daughter, but Brandie had told her that Hicks had not caused the bruising. Ann knew that Hicks could be verbally abusive, however, as she had heard him abuse Brandie when she was on the telephone with her daughter. She said that Hicks made Brandie stay at home when he was at work, and she was not supposed to let anyone at work know that she was living with him.[163] Of course, Lynn Willette, Louise Robertson and possibly other women Hicks had dated or lived with had also worked with him at the motel.

By the end of the year, Ann had heard through a family member that Hicks was beating Brandie—he had kicked her in the ribs and was otherwise abusing her. The family member talked to Zamboni. She informed him that Brandie was only allowed to call at certain times and that Hicks, while drunk, had taken Brandie to a certain location and told her, "This is where I took the girls and this is where they still are." He later, when sober, denied any wrongdoing.[164]

Zamboni met with Brandie and tried to warn her about Hicks and his background. But, he recalled in 2009, "I got nothing. So I got the Brewer PD to pick her up. She filed a complaint…Hicks is 'going crazy'…But he can't stay away. This is a lot of pressure on the guy, it's pressure, but it's friendly pressure, strange pressure." He compared Hicks to a moth that simply could not stay away from the flame.[165]

Hicks threatened to sue the *Bangor Daily News* and two local television channels in 1997 for stories involving him and his female partners. He continually felt harassed, as law enforcement followed his every move and searched for bodies with cadaver dogs, on foot and on horseback. The Maine State Police, Newport Police Department and Brewer Police Department simply hounded him any way they could. Stories in the press heightened the issue.[166]

Brandie stayed with Hicks and became pregnant the following year. The Maine Department of Human Services got involved and removed the baby girl, Hillary,* from Brandie's home in 1998, in large part because of her relationship with Hicks. The state, through DNA testing, proved that Hicks had fathered the child. The baby was placed in foster care soon thereafter. Mayo had for some time denied that Hicks was the baby's biological father, and she even denied having a sexual relationship with Hicks. As Hicks himself had denied being the father, Brandie was quite likely following his lead.[167] By this time, Hicks would have been forty-six years old. He was a convicted killer, and Mayo and Hicks had a stormy relationship.

Brandie married Hicks in Bangor in November 1998. The couple resided in a motel for a short time and then moved to First Street in Bangor—just off Route 2—for a brief period. Brandie conceived another child with Hicks. Before that baby, Ian,* was born, the couple had moved to Texas, seemingly to avoid having the Maine Department of Human Services remove Ian from their custody.[168]

At about the time Hicks decided to move, Maine law enforcement took the Hicks cases to the Federal Bureau of Investigation. The Newport Police Department and the Maine State Police provided information, and the FBI's Critical Incident Response group assigned to the National Center for the Analysis of Violent Crime (NCAVC) analyzed Hicks and his activities. The FBI held a case consultation on June 15, 1999, at the Boston Division of the FBI.[169]

Based on the case materials submitted and the Boston consultation, NCAVC determined that "James Hicks is likely responsible for the disappearance of both Jeri-Lynn [*sic*] Towers and Lynn Willette." Furthermore, the FBI team determined that "James Hicks has been involved in at least three incidents in which females who he was associated with at the time of their 'mysterious disappearance' have never been seen nor heard from since." Although Hicks had served time in prison for his part in Jennie Cyr's disappearance, the report stated, "It is quite obvious by his subsequent actions that this incarceration did little to alter his pattern of behavior." In sum, the FBI "strongly" opined that "James Hicks will continue to pose a genuine threat to a variety of female acquaintances until he is stopped by law enforcement or otherwise."[170]

The unit also stated that "Brandie Mayo should be extremely cautious of her current situation and…law enforcement is perhaps obligated to once again advise her of the past history of James Hicks." The FBI made suggestions as to how this might be done, as well as recommending other possible law enforcement actions, including short-term surveillance and possible long-term undercover activities aimed at securing information on Hicks's criminal activities. The NCAVC supported having the Newport Police Department and Maine State Police travel to Texas to meet with law enforcement personnel there.[171]

After a discussion between a few interested parties, Chief James Ricker of Newport said that he had no qualms about informing Texas of what had been going on in Maine. He said that he would contact Texas authorities and outline the basic facts as known to date.[172] Maine did not want to lose its prime suspect in two unresolved cases.

Ricker wrote to Levelland chief of police Ted Holder on June 20, 1999. He started his letter by saying that he wanted to "apologize for sending one of my worst citizens south to your community." He wrote that he was "the Chief of Police in a small country town in mid-Maine" and that soon after he was hired in 1982, the department had received a missing persons complaint regarding Jerilyn Towers. This complaint, he continued, turned out to be much more "than a simple missing person case."[173]

Ricker went on to state that James Hicks's name had surfaced "almost immediately" in connection to the case, and he described how the investigation had instigated a second investigation into the disappearance of Hicks's first wife, leading to Hicks's conviction of fourth-degree murder. He noted Hicks's suspected involvement in the disappearance of his girlfriend Lynn Willette. He informed Chief Holder that in June 1999, Hicks and his wife had moved to Levelland. The State of Maine had removed the couple's first child in 1998, and the young woman would soon give birth to another child. Ricker wrote that the FBI had identified Hicks as a serial killer even without the discovery of bodies. He informed Holder that he would like to meet with him and other officials to discuss possible law enforcement actions, as "we sincerely feel that Mr. Hicks will kill again and almost any female could fall victim." Ricker had already spoken with Corporal Eddy Burton of the Levelland police force and sent him various documents.[174]

Maine State Police detective Joseph Zamboni played a pivotal role in pursuing Hicks after he moved to Texas following Lynn Willette's disappearance and in bringing him back to Maine in 2000. Shown here in Portland, Maine, in 2009, Zamboni retired from the Maine State Police in 2004 and soon began another career teaching criminology. *Photograph by Trudy Irene Scee.*

While Texas law enforcement considered the Maine communications, Zamboni traveled to Texas to testify in the child removal case. Primarily at issue was Hicks's history and how he had treated women and children over the years. As Brandie had continued to have a relationship with Hicks, her maturity and reliability also came into question.[175]

Hicks's psychological evaluation diagnosed him as having disruptive "psychotic behavior" and probable "delusions of persecution." He was "angry, resentful, prone to hostility, and projects blame onto others." He was likely to feel that he had gotten a "raw deal" and have "periods of overly paranoid behavior." He was judged to be reclusive, probably shy, an introvert, "unlikely to seek treatment, and unlikely to cooperate in any treatment he might receive."[176] The outlook for a stable home environment did not look good, and the State of Texas, alerted to events in Maine, brought a permanent removal case against Brandie and James Hicks that went to trial on April 4, 2000. The State of Texas requested that Joseph Zamboni provide testimony about James Hicks's background and the criminal investigations regarding him.[177]

By mid-April 2000, James and Brandie Hicks had lost two children to the government, and they had a third on the way. Then, just a few days after the State of Texas removed their second child, James Hicks attacked a Texas woman.

CHAPTER SEVEN

THE ONE WHO GOT AWAY

The Case of June Elizabeth Moss

J une Elizabeth Moss was sixty-seven years old in April 2000. She lived in Lubbock, Lubbock County, Texas. She needed some work done on her home and called contractor Danny Hines about it. He and his workers—one of them James Hicks—painted the exterior of Moss's house in October 1999. June, however, wanted additional work done.[178]

June noted that Jimmy Hicks was a good worker and asked him if he did any work on the side. He said that he did, on weekends, when he was not working for Hines. Hicks, however, was apparently not upfront with his employer about some of this work. He told Moss that he did not want Hines to know that he might work privately for her.

The two reached an agreement, and a week or two later Hicks and his fourth wife went to the Moss residence. Hicks painted the outside window metal trim, and June told him that she also needed some work undertaken inside the house. She paid him $100 for the completed work and agreed to pay him $750 to paint her inside walls and $250 to lay tile in two bathrooms. Hicks painted one or both bathrooms and some cabinets. Then, due to a family illness, Moss was unable to arrange a time for Hicks to finish the project.

Just after the custody trial in which he lost his son Ian to Child Protective Services (CPS), Hicks called June Moss and told her that he could come over that weekend, April 8 and 9, 2000, to finish the work. He arrived at her house that Saturday morning and told her he was going to go purchase the necessary paint and bathroom tile. He took two empty paint cans—one for wall color and another for trim—to match at the paint store. Moss gave him a check for $463 for the paint and tile. Hicks planned to cash the check at a local branch of the Bank of America.

Hicks called June from the bank to tell her that the account from which she had written the check was closed. He asked her to come to the bank with another check. She did, and the bank cashed that check. She gave Hicks the cash. Hicks said that he would pick up the paint and the tiles and meet her back at her house. Unfortunately for June, that's exactly what he did.

James Hicks would later agree with much of June Moss's story, up to the point where he bought supplies for repairing her house and met her back at her house later that day. At that point, two widely divergent stories develop.

James Rodney Hicks did go to pick up paint for June's house. He supposedly also bought the tile but told June that it would not be delivered until Monday. Hicks returned to the Moss household, backed his van up to the garage door and unloaded the paint.

While they were outside, Moss noticed that Hicks was drinking a beer. He asked her if she minded, and she told him that she did not want him drinking in her house. Hicks told her that even though he had wasted most of the day running around for supplies, he would start on the project right away.

Moss went into the house and sat down. She heard her front door open and close and saw Hicks bring in a blue bag. Hicks came over to June and stood in front of her. He was holding a gun in his right hand. He said, "This is real" and "I'm not going to f---ing work for you anymore."[179]

"Jim's whole personality had changed," Moss stated. "He was red in the face and angry. Jim made me give him my glasses. Jim was talking very loud, and usually he is soft spoken. I tried to stand up, and Jim pushed me back down in the chair."[180]

Hicks then went on a tirade about the job and about his life. He told her that he was not able to see his son anymore because "CPS took him away." He said, "I'm not going to finish this f---ing job. It's taken too long. I should have finished a month ago but I've had problems and you've had problems but I've got to get out of here."[181]

Moss tried to use a nearby telephone to call for help, but Hicks grabbed the phone and yanked the wires out of the wall. He wrapped the cord around the telephone and placed the phone on Moss's couch. He then locked the doors to the house, disconnected the kitchen telephone and ripped out the bedroom telephone wires.[182]

Hicks continued his disjointed monologue. He told the silver-haired woman, "I've been married four times and I killed my second wife and did ten years in Maine…and I'm not going back there. I've got to get out of town, out of state, but it takes four f---ing hours to get out of Texas." Hicks continued, "I'm not going to kill you because I like you, and besides, in Texas they put you on death row."

The One Who Got Away

Hicks grabbed June by her arm and told her to get up, she was going into the bedroom. She told him, "No, I don't want to go in there, let's stay in here." Hicks yanked her to her feet, yelled at her and then fired his gun.

As Moss described it:

> We walked to the bedroom and he told me to sit so I sat down on the side of the bed. Jim wanted to know if I had any money, and I told him I don't have very much money. Then he asked me about jewelry and I told him he could have whatever he wanted, just don't kill me.

Hicks ordered June to go back to the den and asked her if her husband had a German luger. She told him no—he had gone to war, but not to Germany. Hicks asked her if she had a pistol. She told him that she did not, but she did have some rifles. He asked where they were. She went with him to a front bedroom and pointed him to the closet where she kept the guns. He sent June back to the den.

June sat down. Hicks came back, locked the front door and told her to write him a check. She informed him that she had written her last check at the bank earlier. He asked her to get more checks. He also reached into her purse and removed three or four dollars.

Hicks then asked Moss how much money she had in her checking account. She told him that she had a little over $1,500. He said, "I don't want to take all of your money, just make it out for $1,250." He asked her to make the check out to "Jim Hicks."

Hicks was looking through Moss's purse during this time and discovered that she had recently cashed a check for $200. He told June that that amount should be about what she owed him for his work on her house. He took the cash.

Next, Hicks asked for the title to Moss's car. She tried to tell him that she did not know where it was, but fearing for her safety, she soon admitted that she did. They went into her home office together to get the title. While there, Hicks saw two dollars and took it.

Back in the den, Hicks asked her to turn over her car title to him. June told him that she would need her glasses back. Hicks took her glasses out of his pocket and gave them to her. When she asked him whose name to write on the papers, he told her, "James Rodney Hicks." The two went outside to ascertain the current mileage on the car, and she sat down and finished filling out the title.[183]

After finishing the transfer of the car title, Hicks had June write a note to her children. He wanted her to write that she was giving him the car, money and other items of her own volition. He dictated, "Dear Susan and Steve, I am sorry but there is nobody to take care of me. I am giving Jim my car and the washer and dryer."[184]

June Moss decided to pull one over on Hicks. When he told her to sign her note to her children, she signed it "June E. Moss," just as she had signed everything else that day. June correctly surmised that Hicks would not notice that she would not have signed her full name to a note to her children. She would simply have signed it "Mom." Hicks asked her to write a second note exactly like the first so that he could compare them. That accomplished, he asked for her driver's license and compared it to her notes. He asked June what else she had in her wallet. She told him she had a few credit cards. Those he did not want.[185]

Hicks started pacing. He then left the room and returned with his blue bag. He took out a second beer and a Coca-Cola bottle. He took the top off the thirty-three-ounce soda bottle and told June Moss to drink its contents. She asked him if it was poisonous. He told her that it was not and took a drink to try to prove it.

As she described it, "Jim gave me the bottle and said, 'DRINK!' I asked him again if it was poison. Jim said, 'No, it's cherry cough syrup and I put a bottle of regular in it.' I asked him again if it was poison and he said, 'No! I got it at the Dollar Store.'"

Moss started drinking the contents of the bottle and then spit some of it out. He yelled at her to drink it. While all of this was going on, Hicks finished his first beer and opened the second. He told Moss to hurry and finish the cough syrup.

Hicks then started on what appeared to be the second part of his plan for June Moss. He left June in the den, went into a bathroom and turned on the water. June was not certain if the water was running into the bathtub or the sink.[186] She would later learn that it was most definitely the bathtub. Moss could not know it at the time, but Hicks's new plan for her, which included a waterproof receptacle, was an extremely ominous development.

James Hicks returned to where the frightened woman was sitting, waved his gun at her and ordered her to drink. He left the room briefly, returned with a stack of washcloths and said, "That was a stupid thing for me to do, to leave you in here by yourself."[187]

June Moss was able to escape from the room and the house when Hicks went to check on the water level in the bathtub. She ran to a neighbor's house. Hicks discovered her missing, went in search of her and then got into his van and drove off.[188]

The One Who Got Away

Two of the neighbors, a man and his grandson, rushed out and followed Hicks. Meanwhile, emergency personnel arrived at the Moss residence and, uncertain of how much cough syrup June Moss had imbibed, transported her to a hospital. Police found all of the doors to June's house locked, sprung one and searched the residence. The bathtub was half full.[189]

The neighbors who had gone in pursuit of Hicks eventually called the police and told them where they were. They described the many places that Hicks had driven since leaving the Moss residence and said that they saw him throw something into a hospital dumpster. Police searched the dumpster and found a gun, a photograph of June's daughter and some torn paper. The paper would prove to be the car title, and the weapon was a Daisy C02 BB gun.[190]

Texas law enforcement quickly located Hicks in Levelland. When police officers arrived on location, they found Hicks sitting in the driver's seat of his van. He had backed the van up to the front door of his house. The van was running.[191]

Officers arrested Hicks on April 10 and took him to the Lubbock County Jail for processing. They recorded his height at five feet, six inches, his weight at 155 pounds, his eyes as gray, his hair as blond and gray and worn in a military cut and his face as clean shaven.[192]

The State of Texas charged Hicks with aggravated robbery of an elderly person. Hicks was held in the county jail while awaiting trial on a $250,000 bond. The court indicted him on Wednesday, April 12, five days before his forty-ninth birthday. Because Hicks was a convicted felon and had used a gun in the commission of his robbery of June Moss, he faced the maximum sentence for aggravated assault in Texas: life in prison.

James Hicks, however, did not find his Texas prison cell conducive to his happiness. Nor did he like the prospect of serving hard time in a Texas state prison. Hicks started to consider his options, just as Maine law enforcement officers considered theirs.

Hicks contacted Don Colson at WABI-TV in Bangor, Maine. By letter, Hicks told the broadcaster that he had a story to tell and asked him, "Do you want to be in the end, middle, or begin[ning]" in getting the story? Hicks also stated, "It will cost you." Colson replied that the station did not to pay for news stories and contacted Joseph Zamboni about the offer.[193]

At the same time, Hicks started sending out feelers to Maine law enforcement regarding his situation in Texas. He initially sent messages to Detective Joseph Zamboni via family members, and Zamboni met with Steve Hicks on April 27, 2000. At the meeting, Steve Hicks related his brother's wish to cut some sort of a deal with Maine authorities, allowing him to serve his prison time in Maine, not Texas. Zamboni told Steve Hicks that

that might be possible, but only if his brother cooperated fully with Maine authorities regarding all past criminal activity in Maine.[194]

The day before Steve Hicks met with Zamboni, James Hicks wrote that he wanted to tell his story—his entire story. But, he stated, he wanted to do it his way and be certain that the "whole truth" came out. He wrote that he had been offered money for his story but that he could not at this point say anything without speaking to his attorney.[195]

The State of Maine realized that events in Texas provided it with the advantage it needed to force Hicks to cooperate with its missing persons cases. Using the Maine Department of Human Services or Child Protective Services had not been enough. When Zamboni learned of events in Texas, he called Bill Stokes and asked him what they could legally do to get Hicks back. "This is the only time we've had enough leverage on the guy," he told Stokes. Stokes had heard from Zamboni from time to time over the years about the case, even when Stokes had temporarily left the criminal division. The two discussed how to best maintain contact with Hicks in Texas and keep their Maine cases moving forward. They soon realized that Steve Hicks—the brother to whom James Hicks remained close—and Hicks's discontent about serving his term in Texas provided the wedges that they sought.[196]

Zamboni contacted Steve Hicks, who told him that his brother was "going crazy" in Texas as "he hated blacks and he hated Hispanics." He was also driving his brother crazy with constant calls and complaints. Zamboni told Steve to have Jimmy call him. Soon thereafter, while he was driving down I-95, Zamboni's office patched a call through from Hicks in prison. Hicks would call many times over the next few months.[197]

On July 17, Hicks wrote to Zamboni and defended his actions in several ways. First, he wrote, "I was going to come back to Maine. To answer all allegations about me. To be extradited without a fight." Things had been going on, however, that displeased him. "Because of J. Ricker. There will be no answers. To the questions you have for me." He was angry about Ricker talking with Vance Tibbetts. He was angry about Ricker purportedly saying that Hicks had had parties with teenagers. "The robbery in Texas was not planned," Hicks wrote. "There are two reasons for what happened here in Lubbock. But like everything else. J. Ricker has f---ed things up again."[198]

Zamboni received a letter from Hicks on July 27, 2000. (This may have been the July 17 letter or a subsequent yet similar letter.) According to Zamboni, Hicks complained of stories about him carried in the Lubbock newspapers. He was particularly upset about statements he attributed to James Ricker. As Zamboni described it, "I wrote Hicks back and told him that I had no control over the Newport Police Chief."[199]

The One Who Got Away

William Stokes wore different hats in the legal prosecution of James Hicks over the years, from preparing motions in 1983 for Hicks's arrest on charges of murder in the absence of a body to helping extradite him to Maine in 2000 to prosecuting him that same year. Currently serving as deputy attorney general of the state of Maine and chief of the criminal division, Stokes is seen here in his Augusta office in 2009. *Photograph by Trudy Irene Scee.*

Hicks may have been concerned about articles such as those that appeared in the *Lubbock Avalanche-Journal* in the weeks following his arrest. The newspaper not only published articles by its own staff, but it also carried stories written by the Maine press, especially those of the *Bangor Daily News.* One April *Avalanche-Journal* article discussed Ricker's 1999 letter to Lubbock police and stated that the FBI had deemed Hicks a serial killer.[200]

In a June article, the Texas paper quoted Ricker as stating that Hicks was suspected in the disappearances of two Maine women, in addition to the death of his wife. Ricker said, "We're just kind of waiting to see what happens there. We've got our own desires and wish list, certainly. These cases will remain active." He added, "Speaking from a personal standpoint, I won't be satisfied until we have some answers."[201]

Perhaps more harmful to Hicks's public image was the Texas paper's coverage of a psychological evaluation conducted on Hicks in August 1999 by Raquel Conreras. Conreras noted that Hicks provided vague recollections involving missing women, and he stated that "women around me just come up missing."[202]

The psychological evaluation referred to by the *Avalanche-Journal* would have been part of the custody hearing regarding Ian Hicks. And, by mid-April 2000, Brandie Hicks—pregnant with her third child and realizing that this baby, too, would face Child Protective Services' scrutiny and possible removal—was having second thoughts about her marriage to James Hicks. She was also trying to regain custody of Ian.

Brandie Hicks told the court and the press that all she had wanted "was for someone to give me some proof" regarding her husband's former crimes. She stated that she had not believed that he was a murderer in the past but that she now had her doubts. Hicks relinquished his custody rights on Thursday, April 13, in Levelland District Court to focus on his impending criminal battles. On that same day, Brandie filed for divorce and an order of protection against her husband. She said that she feared for her own safety and for that of her children. Hicks said that he would fight neither the divorce nor the protective order.[203] He was drawing his defense lines elsewhere.

CHAPTER EIGHT

A MAINE MURDERER GOES HOME

James Hicks Leads Authorities to Three Bodies

While the press covered events in Texas and connected them to cases in Maine, and while Brandie Hicks considered her options, James Hicks contacted Detective Zamboni a number of times by letter and telephone. According to an affidavit written by Zamboni, by mid-August 2000 Hicks had let him know that he wanted to give a statement about his Maine crimes but would not do it in Texas "because he doesn't trust anyone down there. He believes if he tells his story in Texas, he will be left in Texas until he dies." Hicks wanted to "serve out his sentence in Maine because he doesn't get along with the Hispanics in the Texas Jail, and his friends and family are unable to visit him in Texas." Hicks had admitted to robbing June Moss and planned to plead guilty to the crime. Zamboni had told him that Maine did not presently have an arrest warrant out for him. When the detective told Hicks that he did not know what Hicks had to tell him, Hicks replied, "You know exactly what I am going to tell you." Zamboni believed that Hicks would "confess to the Lynn Willette murder (and possibly others) if and when he is brought to Maine."[204]

Zamboni began taking steps to travel to Lubbock to make an acceptable deal with all concerned parties regarding James Hicks and his crimes. He flew to Texas on Wednesday, September 27, 2000. The following day, he interviewed Hicks at the Lubbock Police Department. Hicks's attorney, Dennis McGill, was also present. Hicks was advised of his Miranda rights, and the interview was both audio and videotaped.[205]

On September 28, 2000, at the Lubbock Police Department, thousands of miles away from the scene of the crime, James Rodney Hicks finally admitted to murder. Not in those words, perhaps, but he admitted to killing Lynn Willette at their Brewer apartment on the Saturday of Memorial Day weekend 1996 and told Zamboni that he would lead him to her remains.[206]

Yet, Hicks retained a sense of aloofness from his actions and tried to give law enforcement as little information as possible. After a few initial questions, the interview proceeded as follows:

> *James Hicks (JH): All I'm gonna say is that I'll admit to a crime in Maine...the missing person case on Lynn Willette, that I do know where she is and stuff like that, but as for giving physical or any evidence at all or anything at this time, I'm* [not] *giving any.*
> *Joseph Zamboni (JZ):Ok, so I take it to mean* [from] *what you just told me is that you are responsible for the death of Lynn Willette?*
> *JH: Do I have to use the word death?*
> *JZ: Yes.*
> *JH: Yes.* [207]

Zamboni asked Hicks how Lynn had died. Hicks evaded the issue as much as possible, only admitting that he had caused her death. Zamboni then had Hicks clarify why he was admitting to knowledge of Lynn's death. The discussion went as follows:

> *JZ: You're not doing this because of the goodness of your heart, you're doing this...because you want to go to Maine to do your time.*
> *JH: Yeah, I want to do my, be sentenced in Maine and do my whole, do my time in Maine, not come back to Texas at all, and when I get to Maine I'll cooperate...and show you evidence and everything...to give you closure on the cases that we talked about, or you know about.*

The detective asked Hicks to be more specific. He said that the attorney general of Maine was expecting more from Hicks than he had given them thus far. He was expecting Hicks to be more forthright, even if he did not yet identify any specific burial location. Hicks simply responded, "Well, why don't I just say that she's dead." He asked Zamboni if that was enough. Zamboni queried, "You caused her death?" Hicks answered, "I caused the death." He also admitted he was the person who had left Lynn's car at the Hermon truck stop.

Hicks assured Zamboni that he could find Lynn's remains—he had not destroyed them. Then, as if to point out a superior strategy on his part, he said:

> *I can show you anything and everything that I know about the cases...You've investigated some of these cases for over 20 years, on*

*no evidence...I've learned by watching television and reading detective
magazines while I was a kid, and talking to people, if you're gonna do
a crime, you do it alone.*

Zamboni then threw Hicks something of a loop. Instead of the three
Maine cases, he asked him about *five* cases. A few other women had come
up missing in Maine over the years, two of them at about the same time that
Jennie Cyr disappeared. Hicks was having none of it. "Five?" he responded.
"There's just three." Zamboni led Hicks to admit that Jennie Lynn Hicks,
Jerilyn Towers and Lynn Willette were the three cases they were talking
about and then asked him:

> *Is it likely, after you cooperate, that the remains of the other two will be
> found also?*
> *JH: What other two?...I don't even know what you're talking about. What
> do you mean, what do you mean the other two?*
> *JZ: When you come to Maine, we expect that you're going to cooperate on
> everything you've done.*
> *JH: Yeah.*
> *JZ: Not just the Lynn Willette case.*
> *JH: Yeah.*
> *JZ: You're going to cooperate on Jennie and Towers.*
> *JH: Yeah.*
> *JZ: Once you get to Maine.*
> *JH: Yeah, I'll cooperate on all three of them.*
> *JZ: The question is, is it likely there would be remains left on the other
> two cases?*
> *JH: Now, see, that's where you're losing me, right here.*

Hicks continued to assert that he did not know anything about any
cases other than the three with which he had already agreed to help. The
detective then stated that the other two were "women that were missing in
the Newport area." Zamboni identified one of the women, Ellen Choate,
and the exchange continued:

> *JH: Yeah, no, the only thing I know about that was what I read in the
> papers.*
> *JZ: You had nothing to do with that?*
> *JH: No.*
> *JZ: Then there was a girl...Leslie Spellman who was hitchhiking on*

Route 2 and was found down on Mt. Desert Island...You had nothing to do with that?
JH: No. I have enough problems with the women I know let alone going out and picking up people I don't know.

Ironically, and apparently lost on Hicks, he had just admitted that he had been involved in picking up a woman, Jerilyn Towers, whom he supposedly did not know, and then killing her.

Hicks provided information on how he had killed Lynn Willette. Zamboni redirected the conversation by asking Hicks if he had killed her at the motel or at the apartment. Although the conversation that followed provided the detective with the information he needed to arrest Hicks for the murder of Lynn Willette, it did not satisfactorily answer all of the detective's questions. Hicks insisted that Lynn had died at the apartment and that she had gone there willingly. He said:

> *Oh, she picked up some mail that came there, one letter from the school and everything. And I told her I could bring it to her like that, and she said she'd come get it. I told her that Friday, I think it was Thursday or Friday, and she said she'd pick it up, cause we, we were gonna be at work Saturday...So she stopped at the house and we talked while she was there, and a, then we went for a ride and everything and we came back and everything it's, one thing led to one thing, to another I guess and I just snapped.*

Zamboni asked Hicks if he had had sex with Lynn that day. He said yes, "but that was willing." Hicks, when questioned, also restated his earlier assertion that he and Lynn had been about to have sex when their landlady came into the apartment and that he and Lynn had gone for a long ride just like he had told police earlier.[208] Police, however, had found no corroborating witnesses or evidence to support that the ride had ever been taken or that Willette had been at the South Main Street apartment on the day she disappeared.

Hicks reiterated that his confrontation with Willette had happened in the apartment, after the ride. Hicks said that the reason they went for the ride was because "Lynn didn't want to get [in] a row when her sister got out of work or something, to go by like that, and see that she was there, cause she already told Lynn, Lynn had told her sister about my past, everything like that." Hicks then made accusations about someone in Wendy's past and said, "Wendy was upset so Lynn figured my past would outweigh hers and get her to forget her problems. And that was one of the things we talked about when we went for a ride."

A Maine Murderer Goes Home

Hicks's statements did not always make sense, nor did they always conform to his previous statements. In another example of this, he said that he had not actually seen Lynn in the Saab on the day before she died; rather, he had read about it. Zamboni disagreed—Hicks had told Zamboni that he had seen them in the car, and he had even told him where the driver of the car lived. Hicks then said that after he heard that Lynn and Wendy had been with that man, he remembered where he lived. A few minutes later, Hicks said that Wendy was planning on divorcing her husband and was interested in a possible romantic relationship with the salesman.

Hicks also said that he did not remember having ever told Zamboni about there being a problem at the motel with a light in one of the rooms or that he had gone back to the office or that Lynn might have forgotten her pocketbook or something else there.

The last word, and the last statement that Hicks made during the interview, was "suffocation." The question had been "How did Lynn die?"[209]

The next day, September 29, James Rodney Hicks pleaded guilty to aggravated robbery, first degree, in the 137th District Court of Lubbock, Texas. District Attorney Susan Scarlaro asked the court to impose a fifty-five-year sentence on Hicks. The court continued the case for sentencing, and Hicks waved his extradition to Maine should an arrest warrant be served on him by the State of Maine. Police returned James Hicks to the county jail to await sentencing, and Joseph Zamboni returned to Maine to begin working on an arrest warrant for the murder of Lynn Willette.[210]

As Deputy Attorney General William Stokes explained in 2009, things moved quickly in 2000 because "we were running into problems with the weather—we needed to get into the ground before winter—plus we needed to be certain Bush would be around to sign the papers." George W. Bush, then Texas governor, was supportive of the extradition of Hicks. He was running for the presidency at the time and was often away campaigning. If Bush won the election, he would be leaving Texas.[211]

Zamboni obtained his warrant on October 4. On October 6, he returned to Texas. Maine State Police detective Ken MacMaster accompanied him, as did Sergeant Chris Coleman. The officers picked Hicks up at the Lubbock County Jail and flew with him back to Bangor. There, Hicks was to appear at the Bangor District Court and again await his fate in the Penobscot County Jail.[212]

As Zamboni reminisced in early 2009, "As soon as we get on the airplane, he's ready to go. We're eating lunch, and he starts talking. He said, 'So, I got this big knife and I…do you want those potato chips?' 'Yes, Jimmy, you can have the chips.' 'So, I just, you know…Can I have those…?'"

James Hicks was incarcerated at the Penobscot County Jail in 2000 after his extradition from Texas. He was held there while leading police to the remains of his murder victims and confessed to his crimes at the jail, shown here from the rear of the facility. *Photograph by Trudy Irene Scee.*

Hicks rambled on to Zamboni during the entire trip back, enjoying the food, the flight and his own stories.[213]

Zamboni also stated in 2009, "When we got back he basically took us everywhere."[214] Hicks's revelations, however, as seen in transcripts of his first days back in Maine and in his subsequent seven-hour debriefing or "confession tapes," were often incomplete, erroneous or conflicting in details, sometimes with one another, sometimes with past statements. Yet, in the end, after much searching, the families of the women Hicks confessed to killing did get remains of their loved ones back. The remains, however, were not necessarily complete.

On Tuesday, October 10, police escorted Hicks from his cell to the new Bangor District County Court building, located on the opposite side of the jail from the Penobscot County Courthouse. The court appointed attorney Jeff Silverstein to represent Hicks. The court charged Hicks with murder and declined to set bail. Bill Stokes—who in 1983 had prepared the motion against Hicks for the case of indictment without a body—was serving at the time as an assistant attorney general and represented the state. An interview was held to establish both Hicks's intent to provide evidence to solve the three Maine murders and that Hicks would serve any prison sentence that resulted from that evidence in Maine prior to serving time in Texas for his conviction there.[215]

After the interview, Hicks left Bangor in the custody of Maine State Police detectives MacMaster and Zamboni. Agent Brent McSweyn, of the Federal Department of Alcohol, Tobacco and Firearms, and Dr. Edward David, of the Maine Medical Examiner's Office, completed the group. In a government vehicle, the men began tracing the supposed route along which Hicks had discarded the remains of Lynn Willette. Zamboni read Hicks his rights at the outset of the journey.[216]

Asked the precise destination for the search, Hicks responded that he could not remember or explain the exact location. "But it's at the other end of Hainesville woods, just before Houlton, and it's almost in Houlton, I guess…I can show you."[217] Hicks thought that he had exited Interstate 95 at Old Town, or Lincoln, and then followed Route 2 to the Hainesville woods.[218] Once again, Hicks had demonstrated his propensity for sticking close to Route 2.

Asked if there had been some sort of landmark by which he might remember his burial site, he said that all he could recall at the moment was that it had been almost at the end of the woods, near a field, "where, I figured the town or somebody has took and made a place where they [made] a dump, [for] salt and everything, you know, dirt from winter…It's a place where the[y] dump the stuff and like that."[219]

Although law enforcement had already learned parts of the story, the ride and interview of October 10 revealed more of the horror of what Hicks had done. By the end of the day, police had a more solid version of what had happened to the three women. The story that unfolded was recorded in the disjointed fashion in which Hicks's testimony and the long ride progressed.[220]

The coroner's office and investigators did not know just what physical evidence they would find on that or following days. The most recent victim, Lynn Willette, had been dead for over four years. Jerilyn Towers had been dead for eighteen years and Jennie Lynn Cyr Hicks for twenty-three. Time, weather, animals and human activity, as well as Hicks's memory and truthfulness, might all influence what they would find. Yet they had to find whatever they could, for the sake of the victims, their families and their friends, and to finally lay these cases to rest. When Hicks started giving them specific information, they had a better idea of exactly how troubling their task would be.

Joseph Zamboni asked Hicks specifically what they might expect to find at the edge of the Hainesville woods. Hicks responded, "You'll find a five-gallon bucket with cement in it with, should have, her two hands and the head in it."[221]

Hicks stated that the bucket would be white, have a cover on it and be "sort of" buried. He said, "I dropped it over the bank and threw some dirt over the top of it. I didn't have no shovel. So that's why I say it's only down as deep as whatever dirt they put over it." He also said, "It woulda sunk in the ground a little bit too, cause it was a little wet."

As to where they might find the remainder of Lynn's body, Hicks responded, "I don't know the names of the roads and everything." As to the general area, he responded, "Well, first place we would probably go tomorrow would be down the Ellsworth Road, out of Bangor heading to Ellsworth on the main drag." That would be Route 1-A. Hicks thought one location was near Jenkins Beach—a public family beach—on Green Lake. Hicks said that they would find Lynn's torso there and, more precisely, her arms and legs. Zamboni then queried, "You hacked her in pieces?" Hicks responded, "Pieces. Well, her legs cut at the joint, at the torso, what do you call it?" He had cut her at the hip on both sides and then cut her arms at the shoulder.

Upon further questioning, Hicks admitted that he had not taken the time to bury what might have remained of Lynn's body; rather, he had put her torso in a heavy-duty garbage bag—as he had her arms and legs—"and dropped it in between" two rocks. He thought that he had put the knife he had used under a flat rock in the same general area. But he then said he might actually have been thinking of an arm and not the knife—one of the two might be in Brewer. He said that he had removed her clothing and jewelry.[222]

Zamboni continued to ask Hicks questions, dragging information out of him as they rode along. He asked how long Lynn had been dead before he cut up her body. Hicks responded, "I'm gonna say three or four days, I guess. The blood in her hadn't started drying up yet."[223]

As for where he had dismembered the body, Hicks said, "At the maintenance shop, as you walk in, straight down, like you're going to the paint room, and after you go past the bathroom there's a little walkway that goes to the left, it's right in there." He said that her body had been in a small wall partition for about a day, a paneled partition through which part of the motel cooling system passed. Hicks had wrapped Lynn's body in a blanket and then wrapped plastic around both.[224]

At this point, Hicks confessed what he remembered of how he had murdered Lynn Willette. The conversation went as follows:

A Maine Murderer Goes Home

The search for bodies in Etna was centered on an area near this outbuilding on the Hicks property on Route 2. Photographed numerous times by the press, this building was not the one that had once "sheltered" one of Hicks's victims. *Courtesy of the Maine Attorney General's Office.*

JZ: You had a confrontation with her and strangled her, correct?
JH: Yeah.
JZ: With your hands?
JH: No, I used a, what did I use? Huh, you got me on that one.
JZ: You don't remember? But you did strangle her?
JH: Yeah, yeah. Think I had something in my pocket, I'm not sure.
JZ: Something like what, a cord, a rope…
JH: Rope or something like that. Cause I was always playing with ropes and stuff.

Hicks again said that he had killed Lynn in the South Main Street apartment, and Zamboni asked him how he had transported her to the motel. Hicks said, "I put her in a wooden box I made for my tools." A co-worker was retiring, and Hicks said that he was going to store his own tools, "cause I didn't want the motel new owners taking over and think they was theirs." So into the storage box he put Lynn's body. The box was about eighteen by eighteen inches by three feet. He said that her body was intact and clothed. He reiterated that the body was at the motel for only about a day and that it had been in the apartment for two or three days, wrapped in a blanket in the bedroom closet. He said that he moved her body late one night after going out to get beer. He said that when he cut into her body, there had been so much blood that he blacked out from the sight of it.

After he regained consciousness, Hicks proceeded with his task and carefully apportioned parts to various bags. He then "mixed up some cement," put some of it into a bucket, placed Lynn's head in it, along with her hands, and added more cement. He disposed of the bloody blanket and plastic in a dumpster at Shaw's Supermarket off Hogan Road in Bangor. He disposed of the bags with Lynn's body parts one day, and then, perhaps the next day, he took the bucket north to the Houlton area.

Dr. Edward David asked a few questions about the body and the route, which Hicks then said included one of the side roads off Route 9, known locally as the Airline Route, beyond Brewer. Hicks said that he was surprised that a hunter or someone else had not found evidence or remains to date.

Hicks then made his story yet more gruesome. He said that he took his girlfriend and later wife Brandie to the Green Lake site a couple of times, although he made it clear that Brandie never knew anything about what he had done or why he was taking her there. He also said that he had driven by the Houlton site once on a weekend by himself. He had not seen any remains or the bucket on those trips.

Those present with Hicks on October 10 moved the discussion to the 1982 disappearance of Jerilyn Towers. In many ways, although he admitted to having killed Lynn, in all three cases Hicks kept himself as removed from the events as possible. Detective Zamboni again took the lead in questioning Hicks and maintained as neutral a tone as he could. Yet, as with his interviews concerning Lynn Willette, it is clear in many places that Zamboni doubted Hicks's stories—or certain details of those stories—about the murders of Jerilyn Towers and Jennie Cyr.

Hicks told the officers that he had talked with Jerilyn Towers at the Gateway Lounge on the night she disappeared in 1982 and that he had bought her and a few other women drinks. At closing time, the two left the Gateway. Jerilyn, he said, was just ahead of him as they walked out. In the parking lot, Hicks had to open his car via the passenger side door, as the driver's door did not open from the outside when locked. He continued:

Towers was standing on the sidewalk, and when I unlocked the door and got out to shut it I asked her if she wanted a ride and she said no, she was going to walk. She started walking towards Flood's Store, down towards the lake that way there. And so I got in the car.

A Maine Murderer Goes Home

Steven Pickering and Chuck Downing of the Maine State Police watch activities unfold as the state searches for the bodies of Hicks's victims. *Courtesy of the Maine Attorney General's Office.*

Hicks drove to the Main Street bridge, noticed that his fuel tank was almost empty and decided to go back to Flood's to purchase more gas. While he was getting the gas, Jeri came out of the store and accepted a ride. He said that they went to the Newport swimming hole and "parked between the sawmill and the lake."

They talked for a while and then, Hicks said, "For some reason I got in the back to get something or do something." She told him to get back in the front. He thought that he had told her to "wait a minute or a second or something like that." According to Hicks, "The next thing I remembered...well I knew that she was strangled...that she was dead. I don't remember doing it."

Zamboni asked Hicks if he knew how Jerilyn had been strangled. Once again, Hicks's memory was vague. He answered, "I think it was a piece of cloth, a rag or something. Don't know exactly. It wasn't done with a rope or anything like that." Hicks then reconsidered and said, "But no, it wasn't no cloth, musta been with my hands like that cause there wasn't no cloth or nothing." Hicks repeatedly exercised a not so sublime use of the passive voice. Things just "were"—they just happened, without much action on his part. But why had he gotten in the backseat in the first place? Hicks said that the only thing he could think of was that he was getting something out of the back, probably beer, because "she" drank beer.

Zamboni dryly stated, "And so, she winds up dead. She's in your vehicle."

"Yeah." Hicks said that the vehicle in question was his Plymouth Fury III. He remembered it being blue, baby blue, with a white vinyl roof. Hicks then described what he had done after he murdered Jerilyn Towers:

> *When I realized what happened…I just like froze for a few minutes and like that. I don't know how long it was, and then I got back in the front seat, made sure she was dead and like that, and I drove, actually drove through Newport…and got on the Ridge Road…Well I stopped there cause I thought she was making a noise or something like gurgling or something, thought she mighta been alive, so I checked to see if she was alive and I couldn't find any pulse or nothing like this, so I put her in the back seat then, laid her down in the back seat. And a, I just drove from there.*

Hicks said that he thought his girlfriend, Linda Marquis, was asleep when he arrived home, but she woke up. He told her that he had to go down to the field or made some similar excuse to get back out of the house. He said that there was some debris nearby, "so I laid her body down the ground beside the woods and laid a bunch of cardboard and wood and stuff like that…over her."

Hicks started to tell the officers that one weekend when Linda and the children were away he went down to the field, not really knowing what he was going to do. Hicks then changed his story:

> *No, wait a minute, I gotta back up here. After I, the night it happened, on the road there in Newport, I put her in the back in the trunk and I drove home and left the next morning and went to work down to Peasant's Island, or Seabrook, can't remember which one I was working at. And go through the security guard gate and come back again without them checking me. And she was in there. Then when I got home that night there, that's when I took her down to the field and left her.*

Jerilyn had been dead for about a week before Hicks cut her up, he said. "Cause her blood was like dried up and, about like Jennie's, it didn't run at all hardly." He said that after he had returned from work the night after her death, he "went down in the field, put her down in the field, put stuff over her, week later came back, cut her up, put her in grain bags and dug a hole and put her in it." He thought he had cut Jerilyn's body up with a knife used for cutting insulation and similar materials, a knife given to him by another man who worked in construction. Hicks said that it was "like a filet knife…or something like that."

The grain bags that he used were probably hemp with a waxy coating. He cut her body into more easily movable pieces and buried the pieces in the bags in a four- by four-foot area. He added, "It's not even that big because, when I dug the hole and like that, I dug it inside of a building where no one could see me." The outbuilding, a pig shed, was no longer standing in 2000. Hicks said that he had buried Jerilyn's body about ten to twelve inches below the ground.

Dr. Edward David again questioned Hicks about specific details concerning the victim's body. He asked exactly what Hicks had done with the remains, ascertaining that Hicks had indeed dismembered Jerilyn's body as he had Lynn's. He asked Hicks what else he had done, and Hicks replied that he thought that he had covered the individual body bags with lime to get rid of any odors. David asked Hicks again if the sites where she had been cut up and where she had been buried were two separate places. Hicks again said that they were but that the two locations were close to each other, an easy walk apart.

Hicks responded to further questioning by stating that he had disposed of Jerilyn's clothing on his way to work "one day." He said he thought that he had stopped in Pittsfield, taken an exit off the highway and put the clothes in a dumpster. He said that there was no blood on the clothing and that she had not been wearing any jewelry. Hicks insisted that he had not removed any jewelry from Jerilyn Tower's body. Perhaps he found grave robbers more abhorrent than murderers.

The discussion then moved to the death of Jennie Lynn Cyr Hicks. Hicks agreed that he and his young wife had been living together in 1977, but he insisted that both children were home, asleep, when their mother died. Previous testimony had established that their daughter Abigail was with Jennie's sister that night. Hicks also contested the time at which the baby sitter said she had arrived home that night, as well as her condition. Hicks said that Susan had come home at about 11:00 p.m., as he had maintained earlier, and that "she was drunk, not drunk-drunk, but you know, she'd been drinking and was about half to ¾ sheet in the wind." She and Jennie had talked for a short time, and after the sitter had gone in to bed, he and Jennie went to their room. Then, Hicks said:

Jennie was standing, I'm gonna say probably three feet away from me, like [at] the foot of the bed, or the side of the bed, and I was standing on the other side [or] the foot of it, and a, she was standing back-to me like that, and then we was talking, like I said, we was talking like that, and the next thing I know, she was lying on the bed, she was strangled.

Again, Hicks used no active verbs, no causation attributed to himself.

Hicks thought that he had used a belt to strangle his wife. When asked what happened next, he said, "Now, it's, they're all, they're all basically the same, it's like, I don't know how, how it happened...I don't remember it exactly...I didn't know what I was doing." Within a couple of hours, however, he had wrapped Jennie in a blanket. By that time, it would have been close to 5:00 a.m. He left for work as usual, with Jennie's body in the trunk of his Dodge Charger RT.

On the way home from work that day, which would have been July 19, 1977, Hicks stopped along the road and backed up so that the trunk was out of sight of anyone else. Then, he "just opened [it] up and [sat] there and watched, looked at her for awhile. And figure[d] out what I was gonna do. I didn't know what I was gonna do." With no immediate answer to his problem, he said, "I just shut the trunk and that's where she stayed," probably until the weekend.

Hicks drove back and forth to work a couple of times with the body in the trunk. One day, he said, "I parked the car in the driveway, [I] think, for day or two, and no one used it, I wouldn't let anyone use it. Took the keys with me." He still had to figure out what he was going to do. "She was the first one, and I done the same thing anyway, cut off her legs off and her arms off and her hands and head." After that, "Her hands and head was in a, in a cement container, it's like a chest, like a cooler."

When queried further, Hicks said that he had cut up Jennie's body on a Friday or a Saturday. Apparently, he had started driving his car again, as he stated that he "stopped on the way coming back from Woodland [at] another place that was a gravel pit like." He said, "I pulled around a place where they couldn't see me and I just laid her out on the ground and cut her up and put her in trash bags." He put the torso in one place, one leg and one arm in another and the other arm and leg in another location. All locations, he stated, were in Carmel, except for that of Jennie's head.

In a rather confusing exchange, Hicks said, "Ahh, everything was buried except for the body. That wasn't buried, that was just, I just dropped it on top of the ground." He said he thought that he had put it in plastic. He was probably referring to the torso, as he then said that he buried "the other pieces" under dirt, four, six or more inches deep. Hicks then admitted to what he had done to Jennie Cyr's head:

JZ: Now the head, what'd you do with the head and hands?
JH: Put in a kinda icebox, with, put cement in it.
JZ: What do you mean by icebox?
JH: Icebox. Like a cooler you lug around.
JZ: Coleman cooler?
JH: Yeah, big one. Chest cooler.
JZ: Chest cooler.
JH: Yeah.

Hicks said that the cooler was white and green and that he would show the officers where he had buried it the next day. They questioned Hicks further. He said the cooler was in the ground, but not very deep, and that there were rocks on top of it. Detective Zamboni asked Hicks if he still knew where it was and if he had gone back to the site. Hicks said that he had been to the place often.

James Rodney Hicks then revealed a detail that, for some people, would add to the horror of what he had done. He said of the cement-encased head, "I know where it is. Matter of fact, I never buried that until, ahh, I think I was back from Madawaska." According to anecdotal evidence, as well as what he later indicated, Hicks did not bury Jennie's head for years. Rather, he kept it in the cooler in various places, where family and friends would come in close contact with it.[225]

On further questioning by Dr. David, Hicks said that he had scattered the remainder of Jennie's body in various places two to three miles apart. He also admitted that he did not know in what town he had placed one part of her body. David then asked if Hicks had "intermixed" any of the bodies. Hicks answered, "Do what?" David explained, "Nobody is where anyone else is?" Hicks responded, "Nobody is where anybody else is." When asked again, however, he said, "No, well, Towers's and Jennie's, Jennie's head and stuff like that and Towers is within probably a couple hundred feet of each other."

Thus concluded Hicks's formal testimony on October 10. The ride, however, continued. Hicks, in the course of looking for part of Lynn's remains that day, did not offer any explanation of why he had killed the women. He told those present that he had loved Lynn Willette and still did. He said that he had also loved Jennie Lynn Hicks, but that they had been having problems at the time of her death. He said that not only did he not know Jerilyn Towers, but they had also not been fighting that night. According to the Maine State Police report for that day, Hicks said that "something comes over him and he cannot control himself."[226]

Later that day, the men located a Department of Transportation gravel turnout on Route 2 at the Houlton/Forkstown town line. Hicks said that he was confident that that was where he had left the five-gallon pail containing some of Lynn Willette's remains. However, the graveled area was larger than what he recalled, and he did not remember seeing a town line sign there four years earlier. After stopping at that location, the officers returned Hicks to the county jail.

The following day, Maine State Police detective Zamboni and Lieutenant Darell Oulette, along with Dr. David, transported Hicks to the targeted search sites for the bodies of the three women. They started interviewing Hicks at 8:30 a.m. as they traveled along Maine roads, adding to information previously obtained. Having failed to locate any of Lynn's remains near Houlton the day before, they decided to search that area again but first drove to Jenkin's Beach. Hicks said the remains in that area should be contained in two or three plastic bags but suggested that cadaver dogs might be needed to locate them. According to Hicks, before he had left remains in the Green Lake location, he had driven past Ellsworth to the vicinity of Marlborough Beach, an ocean inlet. He said that while he was driving around with Lynn's remains, he drank a couple of root beers and five or six beers and went through a road check. He went to Marlborough Beach, turned around and returned to Green Lake. All of this, he said, was done during daylight because "people notice too much at dark." He further described leaving remains along the beach road, none of it buried, but rather "more or less just dropped on top of the ground."[227]

Hicks also stated during that morning that he might have put cleaning rags that he had used after dismembering Lynn's body behind a tree near Brewer. The knife (a "regular" one from Doug's Shop N' Save supermarket) might be in the Green Lake area, or it might be near Stetson or Exeter, both of which are on the other side of Bangor.[228]

That afternoon, after searching for Lynn's remains in Hancock and southern Penobscot Counties, the group began a search for Jerilyn's and Jennie's bodies, or at least made an effort to identify sites so that a more exhaustive search could be undertaken in the following days. The group traveled to Clifton and Carmel. They looked at a gravel pit on Route 69. They went to a location on the Homestead Road, one on Mount Pleasant Road and one on Lapoint Road. Outside of the Carmel area, they looked at a possible site near Route 9 on the way to Woodland. When asked if he had used the same type of cement in the cooler for Jennie's remains as he had for Lynn's, Hicks responded, "No, I used regular cement there. That was before I knew anything about that stuff." Thus concluded another interview and most of the day's search.[229]

A Maine Murderer Goes Home

Detective Joseph Zamboni (left), former Maine State Police chief Mike Sperry (center) and Maine State Police detective Steve McCaustin (right) at the Etna burial site, standing by a Maine Crime Scene van as the work proceeds. *Courtesy of the Maine Attorney General's Office.*

However, law enforcement did find something before they escorted Hicks back to his cell. At the last stop of the day, at the Hicks property in Etna on Route 2, Hicks directed them to an apple tree. He said that he had buried Jennie's head and hands nearby, in the backyard. He also pointed out where an old pig shed had once stood and said that Jerilyn's remains were located there. Detective Dave Preble, along with Dr. David, made several attempts to locate the cooler. They found a cement block whose surface was shaped like the inside of a cooler. Law enforcement excavated the block and transported it to the criminal investigation office in Bangor. They returned Hicks to jail.[230]

The following day, October 12, officials excavated the Towers site on the Etna property. They discovered a complete set of remains. As Hicks had stated, the body had been dismembered and placed in grain sacks. Officials transported the remains to the medical examiner's office in Augusta.[231]

Joseph Zamboni released the cement block found on the Hicks property to Dr. David for transport to the medical examiner's office on Friday, October 13. That same day, the medical examiner performed a post mortem examination on the remains located on the Etna property. Careful examination did show the remains to compose an entire skeleton. Medical staff also chipped apart the cement block and discovered a human skull but no hands. Zamboni attended the medical examinations.

In the meantime, the search for Lynn's remains in the Houlton area continued, with excavation equipment. On orders, Zamboni moved his search for a bucket from the area identified by Hicks but found nothing. Then, as William Stokes described it:

The police were there for a couple of days. There was a neighbor there, a local, just watching. He never said anything. After everyone left, he wandered

Law enforcement officers excavate a site in northern Maine, looking for the remains of Lynn Willette. The press also photographed this site, which was near where the remains were later located. *Courtesy of the Maine Attorney General's Office.*

over, found two buckets, and called the police and said, "I think I've found what you were looking for."

Indeed he had.[232]

Sergeant Coleman informed Zamboni of the discovery of the two five-gallon plastic pails in the gravel area identified by Hicks and transported them to the medical examiner's office. Coleman attended the post mortem on the remains found in the buckets—a head, two hands, two feet and a tattoo on an excised piece of skin.[233]

The contents of the pails had been examined by late Saturday, and planning continued about how best to proceed with the search. On Monday, David, Preble and Zamboni escorted Hicks to areas that they had previously visited in Carmel and Orrington. They wanted to pinpoint additional, or more precise, search locations, but despite further searches, they found no further remains of Lynn Willette or Jennie Cyr.[234]

The press and some interested parties had attended at least parts of the searches and excavations. Those who witnessed parts of the excavations included friends and family of the deceased. For some of them, it was one of their worst experiences yet.[235]

CHAPTER NINE

CONFESSION AND CONFRONTATION

Three Maine Women Are Laid to Rest

On Thursday, October 26, authorities held a debriefing of James Rodney Hicks at the Penobscot County Jail. Those present that day—Detective Joseph Zamboni, Deputy Chief Medical Examiner Edward David and Assistant Attorney General William Stokes—tried to draw additional information from Hicks, especially information about how and why he had killed the three Maine women and whether he had killed any others. Hicks's attorney, Jeffrey Silverstein, was also present.

Hicks sat in the interview room in an orange jumpsuit, his hands and feet shackled together, his hair neatly trimmed. He laughed and flirted with the camera, stretched and pulled on his shackles and looked down from time to time when discussing what he had done. His demeanor through most of the day was neither one of shame nor remorse. At times, a glimmer of recognition of the depravity of what he had done, of how many people he had hurt, may have flickered through his eyes or his downcast head, but perhaps not; his body language may have been more performance than reality. His conversation was generally relaxed, and he related events with little more concern than other men might have shown when speaking of a family picnic.[236]

Stokes, for the attorney general's office, and Zamboni, for the Maine State Police, did most of the questioning that day. They asked Hicks not only about Jennie, Jeri and Lynn, but also about June Moss of Texas. Hicks had a fair amount to say about each of these women.

As to what had happened at June Moss's house in Lubbock, Hicks denied that he had had any intent to hurt her. He also denied some of the other allegations that she and Texas police had made against him. He stated that on that April day, he had had Brandie and their children on his mind. He had been upset about the recent child custody hearing regarding Ian and the baby who was on the way. He said that he had unloaded the house paint, asked Moss if he could drink beer in her house and went into the living room. He said, "That's when I told her about CPS. For some reason I told her about my history." He also said that for some reason he had brought his BB gun with him. He had just bought the gun that day "because I've always wanted one." He was frustrated that he had been running errands all day and that he would not finish the job that day, but he knew that he had to get out of there. He said to himself, "Oh, f--- it," and the mayhem began. He said he told June that he would not hurt her as long as she gave him money. She did not have "enough" money with her, but she told him that she had some jewelry.

Then, Hicks said, "The BB gun went off." They went into the bedroom. Moss showed him some jewelry, but Hicks told her that the jewelry was not "any good" for him.

When asked about the cough syrup that he had made Moss drink, Hicks stated, "I had it in my bag." But Hicks became frustrated at his debriefing and asserted, "She said I had her write a suicide note…why would I?…She said I made her write a $1,200 check, why would I if I couldn't cash the $465 check?" He then explained, "I had her drink some of the cough syrup because I thought it would give me a couple of hours to get away." He said that he then went into the bathroom and turned the water on. "I came out and she was gone."

Hicks denied having locked the front door and said that Moss had not had to unlock it to escape. He admitted that he went out to look for her after she left and that he had his gun on the seat beside him in his van. He then went to get some gas, ran some errands and went home.

Stokes asked Hicks, "What was the purpose of it?"

Hicks responded, "I was trying to come up with a way out of Brandie's life." He said that he did not want Brandie or "the kids" to know about it, but, as he explained, "I loved Brandie in a way, but I know she wouldn't have stayed away from me." And if Brandie Hicks did not stay away from James Hicks, she would not be able to keep the children.

Apparently unsatisfied with that answer, Stokes asked, "Why didn't you just leave her?" Hicks gave essentially the same answer—they would not have been able to stay away from each other. Hicks contended that Texas had nothing against him and that they (or she) were getting the kids back. (After Hicks's arrest, with the major issue removed, it appeared that Brandie would indeed get Ian back from Child Protective Services, and she was able to keep her new baby, Judith.*) Hicks never did get to see his youngest child—he was already in jail when Judith was born.

Confession and Confrontation

Hicks stated that at the time he assaulted June Moss, he had been contemplating suicide, thinking of driving his vehicle into a nearby body of water. "But I couldn't go through with it," he said. He said he drank some beer while contemplating the act—beer laced with cough syrup. Yet Hicks had not killed himself, and it was June Moss who was attacked and forced to drink a cough syrup mixture.

On October 26, Hicks had to discuss more than his Texas assault; he also had to discuss his Maine murders. Much of what Hicks related that day had already been obtained through previous interviews and the recent investigation and body searches. Some details contradicted previous statements or were simply incomplete. Hicks discussed what he had been feeling at the time of the murders and what he currently felt about the women and their deaths.

Hicks admitted to having killed Jennie with a belt, Jerilyn with his hands or his arm and Lynn with a thin string or cord. He killed the women when they had their backs to him, strangled them in one way or another and, after the passage of several days, dismembered their bodies. And all for no particular reason.

James Hicks was charged with murder at the Maine District Court in 2000 for the deaths of Jerilyn Towers and Lynn Willette. Much of the subsequent legal process would also occur here. *Photograph by Trudy Irene Scee.*

About Jennie, Hicks said, "I had a belt on at the time." He took off his belt, wound it around her neck and strangled her. "And the next thing I remember she's dead." He said that he had "messed around on Jennie" for a year or two and that when his son was born "I changed, that's when I knew I wanted to be there." He did not know why he had killed Jennie, just like he did not know why he had killed the other two women. At one point in the hours-long interview, Hicks said, "It's like I do it without a reason."

Hicks reiterated that Jennie had done nothing wrong, and he said that he had not even known Jerilyn Towers—whom he kept referring to as Tibbetts—and that she had done nothing to anger him. However, he said that his wife Linda Marquis Hicks had infuriated him and that he had thought about killing her, blowing her up, but not in a serious way, rather in spite because "she runs her mouth off."

"Lynn was the one who really haunted me," he said of Willette. "I always think of Jennie, because of the kids," he said, but Lynn was the one he felt strongest about. "Lynn's the hardest…it's not that I didn't love Jennie, I did." But, he said of Lynn, "It seemed like she knew me, how to make me feel better, [and it was] the same thing with her." He said again, as he had just after she disappeared in 1996, that when they had sex was "up to her." He asserted that Lynn left him to stay with her mother because her mother had fallen down and hurt herself. He said that Lynn had had a hard life and that one guy she lived with had "almost beat her to death." In response to a question from Zamboni, Hicks said that their talks about Jennie and Jerilyn "didn't bother her a bit."

Hicks admitted to killing Jennie yet remained angry about "the lies" told to convict him. Hicks insisted that "99 percent of" the evidence leading to his earlier murder conviction and subsequent events "was all lies." He asserted of Newport police chief James Ricker, "I knew he was lying, but I couldn't say so…I couldn't implicate myself." He said that Ricker had "pissed" him off from day one. He stated that Ricker had continually lied about him and had given information to the Tibbetts family that he should not have.

As for any previous mention of truck drivers, Hicks said that he had never said anything about his victims having anything to do with truck drivers. He said that Lynn was the only one he knew who had had anything to do with truck drivers. Jennie did not know any truck drivers, and he did not know if Jerilyn had known any truck drivers.

Seemingly, his anger over Ricker, some family members and his prior conviction delayed any confession that Hicks might have made earlier. Hicks stated, "Joe doesn't know how many times he came close to having me tell him about it." He said that he did not get any enjoyment out of killing. He did not know what had come over him when he killed—the women had been alive one moment and dead the next. He said that thoughts of Lynn had always remained with him and that Brandie had been aware that he still felt strongly about Lynn. He said that eventually, before he died—or at least if he knew that he was dying—he would have confessed. Yet, Ricker's actions had apparently made him determined not to cooperate with the police. Hicks explained, "When he made that comment to me that he was going to get me one way or another...well...jacks---," he was not going let that happen.

Hicks offered other critiques of law enforcement officers. He said that police could have caught him sooner had they treated Jennie's disappearance differently. They could have solved two of the murders if they had entered the houses with search warrants for Jennie and Lynn, but in "Tibbetts's" case, he admitted that it would have been harder. He said that law enforcement has to "treat missing persons like a violent crime." He also said, "The only way you're going to prevent it is [through] the family or something." He then contradicted himself, noting, "It's just that it could happen to anyone, anyone could snap or black out and do what I did."

Hicks even goaded his favorite law enforcement officer, Joe Zamboni, to some extent. He pointed out that after he had decapitated and dismembered Lynn, he had put the buckets containing some of her remains in a row with similar buckets at the motel. He said, "You'd been there a few times and they were still there." He had taken the buckets north that summer, two to three weeks after Lynn died. Again, a contradiction of his earlier statements.

As for his return to Maine to help authorities find the remains and face sentencing, Hicks offered some explanation. He said that after Zamboni came to Texas, he realized that he was facing forty to fifty-five years in jail there and that he would be about seventy years old when he got out. And, he said, "I'm not going to live that long." He admitted that he had had problems in Texas while in jail, but not physical issues. He said, "I wasn't black, and I wasn't Hispanic, and I didn't talk Hispanic." He also wanted to be closer to his children and family in Maine.

Stokes asked Hicks, "Is there anything you want to say to the families?"

Hicks replied, "I'm sorry for the victims especially, the families and my family...I'm sorry...I may not show my emotions." He stumbled verbally and then said, "I'm sorry for the pain and that they had to wait so long." He said that he did not want to face any of the families. "I don't really want to face them, the only ones I want to face are my children."

As to why he killed the women, Hicks repeated that he could not understand it himself. He said that he was not angry at any of the women at the time he killed them. In addition to his other contradictions, explanations, criticisms and ironies, he also said, "I don't want to see anyone else get killed and their family go through what I put them through. It's not fair." In this limited way, Hicks admitted publicly that he remained a threat to society. Days earlier, Zamboni had convinced Hicks that he did indeed remain a threat, and if he was not convicted for life, other women would die. Hicks told Zamboni that he was right.[237]

Hicks said that he just knew certain things. He said that when his mother died, around the same time that Lynn disappeared, "I knew she was going to die, I didn't know when…It's like, I knew it." He said that growing up he had had dreams, he would stare off into space, he would "get a vision" about something and when something was happening in "real time," he would have "a feeling" like he "had already seen or done it." He said that he had experienced something like that on the plane with Zamboni while they were headed to Maine. "It's like this funny feeling, it's like I'm drifting off, light headed, I'm there but I'm not." This had happened to him with Jennie and with Lynn. He did not have pre-murder visions of killing them (or Jerilyn), but afterward, he had felt something akin to going back into his body. He said, "It's like from then on I knew exactly what I had to do…like I knew I had to go back to the motel and get the bike." (This would have been after Lynn's death—after he left her car at the truck stop, he bicycled back to Brewer.) As if to support his "vision theory," he asked, "Why did I know to get a sharp knife, ten inches or larger, why did I always know exactly where to cut?" As if it would prove the power of his visions, Hicks testified that he had not had experience butchering animals when he was younger. But at one point in October, when he was asked how he had known how to cut the women, he replied, "I just followed the bones."[238]

The state still had questions about whether Hicks may have killed other people. He asserted that he had not. He said, "I've done three. I've made my quota…I'm not going to do anymore." And, he added, he was not going to take the blame for anyone else's crimes.

Stokes informed Hicks late that afternoon that he would be indicted on November 6, appear in court on November 17 and be sentenced on December 4. The state's DNA confirmation of the victims' identities would come in four to six weeks. After his sentencing in Maine, he would be returned to Texas for sentencing. Hicks said that he wanted Zamboni to be the person to take him there and requested that, if possible, he be sentenced *in absentia*.[239]

Hicks was indeed indicted on November 6 and appeared before the court on the seventeenth. He pleaded guilty to the murders of Lynn Willette and Jerilyn Towers before Superior Court chief justice Andrew Mead. Prosecutor William Stokes and Attorney Jeff Silverstein represented the State of Maine and the defendant, respectively. Stokes spoke of the brutality of Hicks's crimes and of the gruesome remains that law enforcement found. Sentencing would occur on December 4. In the meantime, family members had the opportunity to prepare victim impact statements.[240]

Maine's serial murderer had confessed and he was soon to be sentenced, but had he told the truth, or rather, the whole truth? Had he told the truth about how and why he had killed Jennie, Jerilyn and Lynn? Certainly, Hicks had admitted to killing the women and dismembering and disposing of their bodies. Yet he had shown little remorse and no true sense of responsibility in his words or his mannerisms. He said that it was hard to see his emotions. Perhaps. Nevertheless, Hicks had said that he had not been angry when he killed the women, yet he had been arguing with both Jennie and Lynn not long before he killed them. Both had been planning to leave him. Lynn, indeed, had already moved out, and Jennie had set a schedule for Hicks to move out. Perhaps instead of threatening to leave him, Jerilyn had simply declined to go with him and that had been enough.

Hicks said that he did not know why he had killed the women and that he had not planned to do so. Yet he had clearly gone back to get Jerilyn Towers, or else his whole story of how she ended up in his car and his trunk was a lie. He admitted that he had gone *back* but said that it had just been for gas.

And had not killing Lynn Willette after she had left him, after she had no reason to be with him, after she had supposedly left work that day, taken a bit of planning? Joseph Zamboni, Hicks's more "pleasant" nemesis, continued to express doubts about where and when Hicks had murdered Lynn. Hicks insisted that he had killed her at the apartment. But Hicks had argued with Lynn the day before, and "in Jimmy's mind she was lying to him," Zamboni stated in 2009. Then Lynn just disappeared. "He had it all planned. They both go to the front desk, check out, then Jimmy says there's a problem." He said he was going to check a circuit breaker and asked Lynn to go out back and check the room. "He meets her there and kills her there, is what I think happened," Zamboni stated. Lynn had already clocked out of work that day—it would have been easy for people to assume that she had also *left* work, when indeed she stayed and died there.[241]

Hicks denied any planning or intent to murder and said that after killing each woman "something" would just "come over" him and show him what to do next. But what supernatural power would lead a man to behead a beautiful young wife and the mother of his children and then keep her head in a cooler in cement for years? What supernatural power would help him murder and dismember Jerilyn Towers and Lynn Willette? Hicks's mystical "something" seemed only to have helped him to hide his crimes and not lead him to any higher standard of morality or ethical behavior. And if it was "something" like *déjà vu*, as he had mentioned in his debriefing, perhaps the second time he experienced it, if not the first, he might have realized that "something wicked this way comes" and put down the knife.

Hicks admitted his brutality yet would not recant some of his earlier testimony, even though it seemed unlikely to have been true, and even though admitting to one or two or twelve additional lies would not have, ultimately, led to a harsher legal sentence. Zamboni later said that by holding on to some of the truth, Hicks may have felt that he had, after all, in some way "won." He felt special when all the media and police attention was focused on him. He had cut a deal—coming back to Maine—that suited him.[242] In some part of his brain, he could hold back part of the truth and be the winner.

At his sentencing, the family members of Jerilyn Towers and Lynn Willette had an opportunity to testify about the murders. Jennie Cyr's family was not anticipated to present statements because Hicks had already served time for her murder, even though Hicks had only just admitted to the crime. An advocate for the victims' rights wrote to Chief Justice Mead in late November stating that Denise Clark and Myra Cyr had not had an opportunity to deliver such statements at Hicks's earlier sentencing and had long awaited a chance to so. They both submitted impact statements. Jennie's sister spoke of how much Jennie had loved her children and was so very proud of them and of how she was always there for her. Jennie's mother wrote of how her husband had grieved every day of his life for Jennie until his death in 1997. She wrote of how Hicks had deprived Jennie's children of their mother and her and her husband of their grandchildren. She wrote that, although losing any child to death was difficult, "to have a beautiful healthy loving mother taken from us in this manner is incomprehensible."[243]

One of Jerilyn Towers's sons, Thomas, sent in a statement. He said that he had not been living with his mother when she disappeared, but he had spent the weekends with her and they had all been together the day she died. He wrote that his mother had been happy about the reunion, yet sad that a relationship she had been in was ending. He suspected that on the night Hicks killed her, "She probably needed a shoulder to cry on." When she stopped to have a drink at the Gateway, "We all said goodnight to mother, not knowing that it would be the last time." During the past eighteen years, he wrote, "I had nothing, other than a 1 percent hope that it wasn't true." Of Hicks he stated, "He deserves to hurt a little."[244]

Jerilyn's sister Jean also submitted an impact statement, although she did not attend the sentencing. She said that her sister had been a lovely woman, one looking for someone to care for her. Since Jerilyn's death, "Life had never been the same, and never will be without her." She wrote that "Jeri did not need to die," that Hicks should have been caught years earlier. "My mom sat by her window every night saying a prayer for her…She would call me every morning just to ask if I had heard anything about Jeri. I always had to say no." June Tibbetts died ten months before Hicks confessed to killing her daughter. Jean asked that Hicks never be allowed to step "outside the walls of Thomaston Prison."[245] Hicks would step outside of those walls a few years later, but only to be transported to the new Maine State Prison in Warren, a few miles away.

Other people also submitted impact statements, including the niece of Lynn Willette. Lynn's niece wrote not only of the loss to herself, but also of the devastating effects of Lynn's death on her mother and grandmother. All of the statements became part of the case against Hicks, whether read aloud in court or not.

On Monday, December 4, James Rodney Hicks appeared before Superior Court chief justice Andrew Mead for sentencing. Mead did not allow Assistant Attorney General William Stokes to read aloud statements by the Cyr family, but some members of the families, including Denise Clark, later made copies available to the press. In addition, Jerilyn's daughter Tammy said in 2009 that she had had Jennie's sister stand beside her in court when she spoke, to represent her family and to make Hicks acknowledge that his actions had affected the Cyr family also.[246]

Tammy Price spoke of her mother in court that day. She talked about how she had missed her mother growing up and what it had meant to be denied her mother's presence. The two had not been getting along very well the day Jerilyn disappeared; indeed, the last time Tammy had spoken with her mother, it had been in anger over their bowling trip that day. Hicks had stolen from Tammy the opportunity to make amends with her mother and to form a better relationship with her.[247]

Tammy also stated that the previous years—all eighteen of them—had been an "endless roller-coaster ride." After looking directly at Hicks and telling him that she would not let him destroy her life, she said, "This is the day the roller coaster stops, and I get off and leave you behind."[248]

The press attended the sentencing, just as it had attended—as much as it was able—the excavations of the burial sites. During and after the court session, the cameras caught Hicks laughing and smiling, not necessarily at them but at little things he seemed to find amusing. And at the end of the

Linda Elston, a good friend of Jennie Cyr Hicks, missed her friend dearly in the years following her disappearance. Shown here in 2009, Linda holds a photograph of her husband and their daughters, Marion and Connie, in the mid-1980s. Soon after Hicks was convicted of Jennie's murder, Marion, a playmate of Jennie's daughter, died of cancer. Linda and Wayne Elston subsequently established the Marion Elston Memorial Fund at Eastern Maine Medical Center in Bangor to aid other children with cancer. They keep photographs of both Marion and Jennie at their Carmel business. *Photograph by Trudy Irene Scee.*

day, he still fought for what he seemed to think remained of his reputation. After the families spoke, he whispered to his attorney that he wanted to speak to Detective Zamboni. He said to the detective, "There was a bunch of stuff they said in there that wasn't true." Hicks was angry and wanted to speak out about it. "I told him to let it go," Zamboni said in 2009. The former detective turned Husson College criminology professor also said that Hicks is "a sneaky slick little bastard" and "a coward." Thus, "The women he could push around or bully, he killed. The tougher women, like Marquis or Gomm that fought back, he didn't kill." Zamboni added, "Jimmy Hicks is not a normal person. When you cut someone up every time, it means something."[249] It does, indeed.

On December 4, William Stokes argued that Hicks's crimes had been premeditated. Justice Mead in turn stated that Hicks exhibited no remorse for murdering Lynn Willette and Jerilyn Towers, and he "showed a predator's ruthlessness." Hicks had treated his victims brutally and subjected them to pain. Mead thereby sentenced Hicks to two concurrent life sentences. Prosecutor Stokes stated that the sentence was a fitting one, albeit unusual. He knew of only one other instance in Maine in which a person had received such a sentence.[250]

Jeffrey Silverstein stated on December 4 that Hicks had cooperated with authorities not only because of what he faced in Texas, but also because Hicks "sought closure for himself, his own family, and the other families." As for there being any benevolence behind Hicks's decision to return to Maine, Stokes stated later that day, "I think it's a bunch of baloney…He didn't come to Maine to save these folks further pain. I don't buy it."[251] Of course, Stokes did not have to "buy it," nor did anyone else. Hicks had stated his reason clearly in his Texas interview—he had returned to Maine so that he could serve his time in Maine, not Texas.

Justice Mead not only imposed two life sentences on Hicks, but he also sentenced Hicks to pay restitution to the Towers and Willette families. This was also an unusual ruling in a Maine murder case, but under current law Hicks could be forced to pay Jerilyn's children for her funeral expenses and up to $15,000 to Lynn's family for their loss. Jerilyn's family did not qualify for the larger sum, as it was provided for under a law applied only to crimes committed after January 1, 1993. The restitution would be taken from Hicks's earnings in prison. As of 2009, monies had been paid, in part or in full, depending on the recipient and the award amount.[252]

Maine soon returned Hicks to Texas for formal sentencing. He appeared in Texas court on January 5, 2001. June Elizabeth Moss delivered a forceful impact statement to James Hicks.

Moss told Hicks, "For over twenty years you murdered, molested, and terrorized innocent people and their families. You committed your crimes without shame and now face the consequences without remorse." She told him that "people will no longer hide from you in fear, but for you there is no hiding place." June told James that God would judge his soul.[253]

Hicks declined to make a statement that day. Although he said that he had not intended to kill Moss, Zamboni stated that he believed that Hicks would have killed her had she not escaped.[254]

The Texas court sentenced Hicks to fifty-five years in prison, as previously agreed, with his time in Maine to be served first. On November 16, 2000, George W. Bush and Maine governor Angus S. King had signed an executive agreement between their respective states transferring Hicks to Maine to serve his sentence for criminal homicide.[255] After his Lubbock sentencing, Texas returned Hicks to Maine.

With his sentencing in Texas, Hicks might have been considered duly judged, but had he truly been condemned for all of his crimes? The courts did not indict Hicks for any deaths other than those of Jeri, Jennie and Lynn. But Hicks was questioned about others. The murders of three young women in particular had come into question over the decades. Two of the women—Leslie Spellman and Ellen Choate—were travelling to Maine destinations, destinations that would have taken them along the Route 2/I-95 corridor, but they never arrived. The third, a teenager, Joyce McLain, was killed near her home in East Millinocket, where Hicks sometimes worked.

Police could establish no evidence against Hicks for these murders, however. William Stokes, now serving as deputy attorney general and chief of the criminal division of the State of Maine Attorney General's Office, stated in 2009 that the state believed that Hicks had not committed any murders other than those for which he had been convicted. "Hicks was adamant" about not having killed any other women. "I don't think there were any others," Stokes said. "We couldn't make a connection between him and anyone else. The three we know he did we could independently connect with him." Zamboni also ruled out Hicks as a suspect in the three murders. Hicks had his own methodology, and it was simply not present in those other deaths.[256] Certain aspects of these or other murders might make Hicks seem suspect, but after all was said and done, the links and evidence were simply not there.

Jennie, Jeri and Lynn suffered death at the hands of James Hicks. June Moss was robbed by and faced possible death from Hicks. The families and friends of his victims suffered from the loss of their loved ones. Hicks's own family also suffered from what he had done. His family, or most of it, had not believed that Hicks had committed murder, right up until he returned to Maine in 2000 and started leading police to his victims' remains. One of his sisters stated in 2000, "We stood by him all those years…We were shocked." She said that her family grieved for his murder victims and their families and that her brother had been a "good kid" until he reached a certain age, "an age where we all had our problems."

And of course, the children of James Rodney Hicks suffered from his actions. Two of Hicks's children were denied their mother from an early age because Hicks had killed her; others had mothers who were troubled by their relationships with Hicks or themselves suffered problems due to Hicks; and a number of Hicks's biological and "adoptive" children were removed by state agencies from their homes, temporarily if not permanently, due to Hicks's relationships with their mothers. Being the biological or adoptive child of a serial murderer inherently posed numerous difficulties—and police believe that Hicks may have fathered up to seventeen children before 2000.[257] Hicks wounded many people besides the women he murdered.

In the years since Hicks killed Jennie, Jerilyn and Lynn, several family members have died. Some did not live to see Hicks permanently incarcerated for the crimes he committed. For others, time has not healed their wounds. More than thirty years after her daughter's murder, Myra Cyr simply said, "It's still too difficult to talk about." Linda Elston, Jennie's friend, said in 2009 that she had never made such a close friend again, as "I was so afraid that something would happen to her, and I couldn't go through that again." Her husband, Wayne, said of Jennie, "I think she was deep down scared of him, of what might happen to her kids. He didn't want her, but he didn't want anyone else to have her either. It's just too bad that she couldn't get away."

Jerilyn Towers's sister Jean said in 2009 that she had felt compelled to keep looking for her sister in the years after she disappeared and that she had often felt her presence with her. When she asked their mother why Jerilyn's presence remained, June answered, "Because she knows you won't give up on her." Jean explained that she could not give up on her sister because, "had the tables been turned, she would have looked for me." Jerilyn's daughter made a most telling statement when she said, "My mother tried so hard to stop drinking... she probably would have succeeded by now." Just as Jennie's children were deprived of having their own mother finish raising them and the chance to see who their young mother might have become, so, too, did Tammy and her brothers miss the opportunity to spend invaluable years with their mother, to watch the changes that life might have brought her—and them. Tammy still has the Dexter shoes that Jerilyn wore on the last night of her life. She also has the lucky penny that her mother had placed in her shoe.[258]

Lynn Willette's father, Vincent, died waiting for her to come home; her mother, Jane Hinks, has since died of cancer. Her friends, like those of the other women, still miss her. Her sister, Wendy Allison, said in 2008, "My sister was very complicated, interesting, she was really loved a lot, and people need to know that." She also said that her sister was a very strong woman and that "she was safe, and then for a few seconds she wasn't."[259] Those few seconds meant everything.

June Moss was able to take advantage of a few seconds when Hicks left her alone. In escaping, she perhaps not only saved her own life but also started a chain of events that enabled the State of Maine to extradite Hicks and locate the remains of the three women he had killed.

In the autumn of 2000, the families of Jennie Cyr, Jerilyn Towers and Lynn Willette laid their loved ones to rest in the manner that they felt best.

Initially sent to the Maine State Prison in Thomaston, Hicks was relocated when the state built its new facility in Warren. Hicks will remain at the Maine State Prison until his death. *Photograph by Trudy Irene Scee.*

Jennie's family buried her under the name Cyr next to her father in Auburn. Jerilyn's family allowed close family members to see her remains and then buried her, wearing her newly repaired mother's ring, next to her birth father, Raymond Tibbetts, in Rome. Lynn's family held a ceremony at their home with a more formal service planned for the future—they could not yet bear to part with the remains it had taken years to recover.

In another state, Hicks might conceivably serve less than his court-rendered sentence, but as Deputy Attorney General William Stokes stated in 2009, "In Maine, life is life." James Rodney Hicks may have made his quota—if indeed serial killers have quotas—but the State of Maine would make its quota also. It would exact its retribution in full measure. There is no parole in Maine. James Rodney Hicks will not walk free again.

NOTES

Chapter One

1. Taken from transcripts of the trial of James Hicks, *State of Maine v. James Hicks*, Docket No. Pen-84-143; see also Detective Joseph W. Zamboni, "Maine State Police [hereafter cited as MSP] Affidavit," April 12, 2000; *Bangor Daily News* [hereafter cited as *BDN*], November 10, 2000; and interview with Wayne Elston, January 28, 2000, Carmel, Maine.
2. Ibid.
3. Ibid.; see also Child Keyppers, "Missing Child's Bulletin" 1980s, as well as photographs and interviews.
4. *State of Maine v. James Hicks*.
5. Ibid.; see also MSP Reports.
6. The location of the Hicks trailer was taken from an interview with Wayne Elston, January 28, 2000. Description recalled from a visit to the site, since condemned.
7. *State of Maine v. James Hicks*.
8. Ibid; see also FBI Investigations, NCAVC—Possible Serial Homicide report, June 24, 1999; on Jennie's cake baking, interview with Linda Elston, February 4, 2009, Carmel, Maine; and "MSP Interviews," Richard Reitchell with Gail Sinclair, December 2, 1982, and Deputy Attorney General Fernand LaRochelle with Gail Sinclair, March 1, 1984.
9. Interviews with Wayne Elston, January 28, 2009, and Linda Elston, February 4, 2009.
10. Ibid.; and site visit.
11. Ibid.
12. Interview with Wayne Elston, January 28, 2009.

13. Ibid.; see also "MSP Interview," January 4, 1983, Detective Richard Reitchell with Dwight Overlock.

14. Ibid.

15. Ibid.; see also "MSP Interview," March 22, 1983, Detective Richard Reitchell with Susan Matley.

16. *State of Maine v. James Hicks.*

17. Ibid.

18. Ibid.

19. Ibid.; see also interview with Linda Elston, February 4, 2009.

20. Interview with Linda Elston, February 4, 2009.

21. *State of Maine v. James Hicks.*

22. Ibid.; see also "MSP Affidavit," Joseph Zamboni, April 12, 2000.

23. Ibid. Any of Hicks's passengers may have stayed in the car at some points, or they may have actually been back at the trailer.

24. Ibid.; see also records for Bangor State Fair, 1977.

25. Telephone interview with James Ricker, January 29, 2009. In 2009, William Stokes and Joseph Zamboni supported the idea that the report was either never filed or lost. Also see court documents for 1984.

26. "MSP Affidavit," Joseph Zamboni, April 12, 2000.

27. *State of Maine v. James Hicks.*

28 "MSP Interview," Richard Reitchell with Gail Sinclair, December 2, 1982.

29. Ibid.

30. Letter from Myra Cyr to Maine secretary of state, February 15, 1978.

Chapter Two

31. Composite from various sources. Information on Jerilyn's good-luck penny came from an interview with Tammy Price, February 20, 2009 (location withheld at Price's request).

32. "Investigation Report," Newport Police Department [hereafter cited as NPD], October 18, 1982; see also additions made to the report, beginning on October 20; and interview with Tammy Price, February 20, 2009.

33. "Investigation Report," additions.

34. "Investigation Report."

35. Ibid.

36. "Missing Persons Information," NPD, April 1999 (reissued to MSP); and interview with Tammy Price, February 20, 2009.

37. "Investigation Report," addition, October 22, 1982.

38. "Statements by Family of Jerilyn Towers," undated report, later sections compiled in mid-1990s.

39. Ibid.

40. Ibid.

41. Ibid.

42. "Investigation Report," addition, October 24, 1982.

43. Ibid.; see also letter on file at attorney general's office; and 1982 NPD reports.

44. "Investigation Report," additions, October 1982 and November 17, 1982.

45. Ibid., November 17, 1982, and attached "Continuation."

46. Ibid., November 18, 1982, and attached "Continuation."

47. Ibid., November 20, 1982, and attached "Continuation."

48. Ibid.

49. Ibid.

50. Ibid.; see also report of November 20, 1982, added by Eugene Robinson.

51. Letter from James A. Ricker to Ted Holder, chief of police, Levelland Police Department, June 20, 1999; telephone interview with Ricker, January 29, 2009; and Ricker interview of February 3, 2009, Newport.

52. "Continuation Report," NPD, November 22, 1982, and attached continuations.

53. Ibid.

54. "MSP Interview," with Susan Matley, December 1982.

55. Ibid.

56. "MSP Interview," with Trudy Levansaller, December 13, 1982.

57. "MSP Interviews," with various witnesses mid- to late December 1982. Names withheld.

58. "MSP Interview," with Fern M. Godsoe, February 2, 1983.

59. Ibid.; information on Godsoe wanting to get rid of the mattress and her living at the trailer came from a telephone interview with James Ricker, January 29, 2009.

60. Ibid.

61. Ibid.

62. Interview with William Stokes, January 26, 2009, Augusta, Maine.

63. Telephone interview with James Ricker, January 28, 2009.

64. Ibid.

65. Ibid.

66. Interview with William Stokes, January 26, 2009.

67. Ibid.
68. Ibid.

Chapter Three

69. "Penobscot Grand Jury Indictment," *State of Maine v. James Hicks*, Docket No. 83-591, Penobscot County, October 4, 1983.
70. See *State of Maine v. James Hicks*," Docket No. Pen-84-143; and "Defendant-Appellant, Brief of the Appellant," Pen-84-143.
71. *Morning Sentinel* [hereafter cited as *MS*], July 18, 1985; see also *Boston Globe*, January 31, 1985.
72. *State of Maine v. James Hicks*, Docket No. Pen-84-143, vols. 1–5, for overview of trial.
73. *State of Maine v. James Hicks*, Pen-84-143. Information for following pages are from the same source unless otherwise noted.
74. Ibid., "Defendant-Appellant, Brief of the Appellant," Pen-84-143, 1–8.
75. Telephone interview, January 29, 2009, juror's name withheld on request.
76. Interview with William Stokes, January 26, 2009.
77. *State of Maine v. James Hicks*, "Defendant-Appellant, brief of the Appellant," Pen-84-143. Information for following pages taken from same source unless otherwise indicated.
78. Ibid.; see also *State of Maine, Appellee v. James Hicks, Appellant*, Supreme Judicial Court Sitting as the Law Court, Law Docket No. Pen-84-143.
79. Ibid.; see also *BDN*, December 16, 1984.
80. *MS*, July 10, 1985.
81. Ibid.
82. *Boston Globe*, January 31, 1985.
83. Ibid.
84. Ibid.
85. *BDN*, July 16, 1985.
86. "Missing Child's Bulletin," Child Keyppers, on file at various agencies and distributed publicly in the 1980s; prosecution records; interviews with Wayne Elston, January 28, 2009, and Linda Elston, February 4, 2009.
87. *Portland Press Herald* [hereafter cited as *PPH*], July 10, 1985; Decision of the Maine Supreme Judicial Court, *State of Maine v. James Hicks*, Decision No. 3858, Decided July 9, 1985.
88. Ibid.

89. *MS*, July 10, 1985.

90. Ibid.

91. *BDN*, July 16, 1985.

92. Ibid.

93. Ibid.

94. Ibid.

95. Ibid.; see also *MS*, July 18, 1985.

96. "Supplement to Certificate of Death, RE: Jennie Lynn Hicks, Item # 24, Continued," July 23, 1985; "Affidavit," James Rodney Hicks, August 12, 1985; *MS*, August 24, 1985; *PPH*, August 24, 1985; and *BDN*, August 24, 1985.

97. *BDN*, August 14, 1985.

98. *BDN*, August 24, 1985.

Chapter Four

99. "MSP NPD, Possible Homicide (Jerilyn Towers)," October 2, 1986.

100. Interview with William Stokes, January 26, 2009. The length of Hicks's incarceration was taken from the attorney general's records. Hicks himself, however, quoted the term more than once in the years following his release.

101. Interview of Karen Hicks Mackenzie by James Ricker and Joseph Zamboni, August 8, 1998.

102. Ibid.

103. Interview with Louise Robertson by James Ricker and Joseph Zamboni, August 19, 1998.

104. Ibid.

105. Report by James Ricker, July 21, 1998.

106. Interview with James Ricker, Newport, Maine, February 3, 2009.

107. Interview with Tammy Price, February 20, 2009.

108. Report by James Ricker, July 21, 1998. Report taken from an earlier continuation report.

109. Ibid. There was one disagreement or typographical error about the time on the report.

110. Ibid.

111. "Release of Control from Linda Marquis Hicks," October 4, 1994; Reports of James Ricker, September 19, 1995 and June 24, 1996; and "Continuation Report," NPD, March 31, 1994.

112. "Continuation Report," NPD, February 1994, exact day not indicated on report.
113. "Statements by Family of Jerilyn Towers."
114. "Continuation Report," NPD, March 31, 1994.
115. Ibid.
116. Ibid.
117. Names and sources withheld to protect the women's identities.
118. The names of the children allegedly abused by Hicks and other information has been withheld to protect the children, as are names of allegedly intimidated witnesses. The allegations were made to police in the 1990s for the most part, and some people interviewed by the author during 2008 and 2009 stated that they had been threatened.

Chapter Five

119. "MSP Interview," Joseph Zamboni with James Hicks, June 21, 1996; see also "MSP Report," Summation of Interviews by Joseph Zamboni, September 5, 1996; interview with Sargent Jay Munson, Brewer Police Department [hereafter cited as BPD], February 13, 2009; 2008 interview with a friend of Willette's from the early 1990s; and *BDN*, October 7, 1996, and November 10, 2000.
120. Ibid.
121. NPD, Report of Police Chief James Ricker, September 5, 1995; interview with Sargent Jay Munson, BPD, February 13, 2009; and *BDN*, October 7, 1996.
122. Sketch by Joseph Zamboni, 1997, and general information from site.
123. See records submitted by Joseph Zamboni during the late 1990s and other documents up to 2000. Alleged health issue withheld here.
124. Undated typing sheet by Willette, circa 1996.
125. Ibid.
126. Typing practice by Willette, circa 1996.
127. Ibid.
128. Narration assignment by Willette, October 5, 1995.
129. Essay by Willette, circa 1995–96.
130. Telephone interview, February 3, 2009. Name withheld on request, but individual is well known to author.
131. Ibid.
132. Ibid.; see also interview of September 2008.
133. Interview with Sargent Jay Munson, February 15, 2009.

134. BPD, "Incident Report," August 29, 1995.

135. Interview with Joseph Zamboni, February 5, 2009.

136. Ibid.

137. "MSP Summary of Interview," February 1, 1996.

138. Ibid.

139. Ibid.

140. Detective Joseph W. Zamboni, "Affidavit," August 2000 (exact day not indicated, evidence based largely on previous reports by Zamboni); see also interview with Joseph Zamboni, February 5, 2009, on his feeling that Lynn left Hicks in part because of his and Tibbetts's hounding of Hicks; and interview with James Ricker, February 3, 2009.

141. "FBI, NCAVC—Possible Serial Homicide Report," June 24, 1999.

142. Zamboni, "Affidavit."

143. BPD, "Incident Report," August 29, 1995.

144. Zamboni, "Affidavit"; see also "FBI, NCAVC—Possible Serial Homicide Report," June 24, 1999.

145. Ibid.

146. "MSP Interview," Joseph Zamboni with James Hicks, June 21, 1996.

147. Zamboni, "Affidavit."

148. NPD Report, James Ricker, August 1996.

149. Zamboni, "Affidavit"; and interview with Joseph Zamboni, February 5, 2009.

150. Ibid.

151. Interview with Joseph Zamboni, February 5, 2009.

152. NPD, James Ricker report, August 1996; and composite of MSP reports for 1996–98.

153. "MSP Interview," Joseph Zamboni with Dennis Wallace, June 3, 1996.

154. "MSP Interview," Joseph Zamboni with Teena Adams, June 8, 1996; and interview with Sargent Jay Munson, February 15, 2009.

155 ."MSP Reports," Joseph Zamboni, June 12 and 19, 1996.

156. "MSP Report," Summation of Interviews, Joseph Zamboni, September 5, 1996.

157. Ibid.

158. "MSP Report," Joseph Zamboni, December 3, 1996. Also see other MSP Reports for late 1996.

159. *BDN*, October 7, 1996; see also telephone interview with Wendy Allison, May 27, 2008.

160. See MSP and BPD reports for this period; and interview with Joseph Zamboni, February 5, 2009.

161. "MSP Report," Joseph Zamboni, December 3, 1996; see also reports of January 27, 1997, to February 13, 1997.

Chapter Six

162. "MSP Report," Joseph Zamboni, November 6, 1996.
163. "MSP Interviews," Joseph Zamboni, October 3 and 22, and December 1996.
164. "MSP Interviews," October 3 and November 23, 1996.
165. Interview with Joseph Zamboni, February 5, 2009.
166. "MSP Interview," with James Hicks, August 21, 1997; "Incident Reports," NPD, September 17 and 18, 1998; MSP Reports, December 3, 1996, and May 18, 1998; and general NPD, BPD and MSP records for era.
167. Zamboni, "Affidavit"; see also Joseph Zamboni, "MSP Affidavit," April 12, 2000; and FBI NCAVC Report, June 24, 1999.
168. Ibid.; see also Penobscot County Vital Records.
169. FBI NCAVC Report, June 24, 1999.
170. Ibid.
171. Ibid.
172. Interview with James Ricker, February 3, 2009.
173. James Ricker to Ted Holder, June 20, 1999.
174. Ibid.
175. Zamboni, "Affidavit"; see also Texas evaluation of Hicks, 2000.
176. Interpretation of James Hicks's MMPI-2 Test, as part of the public record for ongoing investigations.
177. Zamboni, "Affidavit."
178. "Witness Affidavit," State of Texas, County of Lubbock, April 10, 2000. The following paragraphs were taken from the same source unless otherwise noted.
179. Ibid.; see also "Lubbock Police Department [hereafter cited as LPD] Case Report," April 8, 2000.
180. "Witness Affidavit."
181. Ibid.
182. Ibid.; see also "LPD Case Report."
183. "Witness Affidavit."
184. Ibid.; see also "LPD Case Report"; and Maine and Texas press during summer and autumn 2000.
185. "Witness Affidavit."

186. Ibid.

187. Ibid.

188. Ibid.; see also "LPD Case Report."

189 ."LPD Case Report."

190. Ibid.; see also "LPD Case Report."

191. *Lubbock Avalanche-Journal* [hereafter cited as *LAJ*], April 15, 2000. Hicks was initially held on a $75,000 bond.

192. "LPD Case Reports," April 8 and 10, 2000.

193. Zamboni, "Affidavit."

194. Ibid.

195. Letter from James Hicks, April 26, 2000.

196. Interview with William Stokes, January 26, 2008.

197. Interview with Joseph Zamboni, February 5, 2009.

198. Letter from James Hicks to Joseph Zamboni, July 17, 2000.

199. Ibid.

200. *LAJ*, April 15, 2000.

201. Ibid., June 2000.

202. Ibid., April 15, 2000.

203. Associated Press article from Levelland, Texas, reprinted in Maine newspapers, April 15, 2000; and *BDN*, April 15, 2000.

Chapter Eight

204. Zamboni, "Affidavit."

205. "Continuation Report," Joseph Zamboni, September 27, 2000.

206. Ibid., September 28, 2000. The following discussion and extracts were taken from this interview unless otherwise noted.

207. "Transcript of Interview," MSP, September 28, 2000, Lubbock, Texas.

208. Ibid.

209. Ibid.

210. "Continuation Report," Joseph Zamboni, September 29, 2000.

211. Interview with William Stokes, January 26, 2009.

212. "Continuation Reports," Joseph Zamboni, September 20 to October 10, 2000.

213. Interview with Joseph Zamboni, February 5, 2009.

214. Ibid.

215. Interview with William Stokes, January 26, 2009.

216. "MSP Interview," with James Hicks, October 10, 2000.

217. Ibid.

218. Ibid.

219. Ibid.

220. See "MSP Interview," with James Hicks, October 10, 2000; and "Continuation Reports," Joseph Zamboni, September 20 to October 10, 2000, as well as other sources previously cited for general overview.

221. "MSP Interview," with James Hicks, October 10, 2000. The following information was taken from the same source unless otherwise indicated.

222. Ibid.

223. Ibid.

224. Ibid.

225. Ibid.; see also "Continuation Report," October 10, 2000; and 2008–09 interviews with Joseph Zamboni.

226. Ibid.

227. "MSP Interview," October 11, 2000.

228. Ibid.

229. Ibid.; see also "MSP Continuation Report," October 11, 2000.

230. "MSP Continuation Report," October 11, 2000.

231. Ibid., October 12, 2000.

232. Interviews with Joseph Zamboni, February 5, 2009, and William Stokes, January 26, 2009; see also "MSP Continuation Reports," October 2000.

233. "MSP Continuation Reports," October 13 and 14, 2000.

234. Ibid., October 14, 16 and 17, 2000.

235. See interviews of 2008 and 2009 and general press for 2000.

Chapter Nine

236. Debriefing videos, James Hicks, October 26, 2000. The following paragraphs were also taken directly from those tapes, unless otherwise noted. Where the questioner is identified by name, it is through voice recognition, as the camera remained on Hicks throughout his testimony.

237. Ibid.; see also telephone interview with Joseph Zamboni, March 12, 2009, on Hicks's admission to him.

238. Ibid.; and interview with William Stokes, January 26, 2009.

239. Ibid.

240. "MSP Continuation Reports," November 17, 2000, and December 4, 2000; court documents; *AJL*, November 18, 2000; and general press for these months.

241. Interview with Joseph Zamboni, February 5, 2009.

242. Telephone interview with Joseph Zamboni, March 12, 2009.

243. Impact statements by Myra Cyr and Denise Clark, 2000; letter from Mary Farrar to Chief Justice Mead, November 30, 2000.

244. Victim Impact Statement, Thomas Tibbetts, November 8, 2000.

245. Victim Impact Statement, Jean Worthley, 2000; and telephone interview with Worthley, January 31, 2009.

246. *MS*, December 5, 2000; and interview with Tammy Price, February 20, 2009.

247. Ibid.; see also Victim Impact Statement, as delivered, December 4, 2000.

248. Ibid.

249. Telephone interview with Joseph Zamboni, May 27, 2008; and Zamboni interview, February 5, 2009.

250. *MS*, December 5, 2000.

251. Ibid.; and *AJL*, December 5, 2000.

252. *MS*, December 5, 2000; interview with Tammy Price, February 20, 2009; and attorney general's records.

253. *AJL*, January 5, 2001.

254. Ibid.

255. "Executive Agreement Between State of Texas and State of Maine," November 16, 2000.

256. Interview with William Stokes, January 26, 2009 (the last quote of the book was also taken from this interview); see also telephone interview with Joseph Zamboni, March 12, 2009.

257. Telephone interview with Joseph Zamboni, May 27, 2008; and interview with James Ricker, February 3, 2009.

258. Telephone interview with Jean Worthley, January 31, 2009; and interview with Tammy Price, February 20, 2009.

259. Telephone interview with Wendy Allison, May 27, 2008.

ABOUT THE AUTHOR

Trudy Irene Scee is a freelance writer and historian. She holds undergraduate degrees in forestry and history, a masters of arts in history from the University of Montana and a doctorate of philosophy in history from the University of Maine. She has also studied engineering and anthropology and has received a number of academic fellowships and awards.

Dr. Scee has taught history at Mount Allison University in New Brunswick and worked extensively for the University of Maine system. For the past few years, she taught at Husson University in Bangor. She has published academic essays, held photographic exhibits and worked as a journalist. In addition to *Tragedy in the North Woods: The Murders of James Hicks*, she has published *In the Deeds We Trust: Baxter State Park, 1970–1994*; *The Inmates and the Asylum: The Bangor Children's Home, 1835–2002*; *Mount Hope Cemetery, A Twentieth-Century History*; *N.H. Bragg & Sons: 150 Years of Service to the Maine Community and Economy, 1854–2004*; and *Trudy Scee's Dictionary of Maine Words and Phrases.* Two additional works are due out in late 2009—one a general book about Maine and one a comprehensive urban history titled *City on the Penobscot: Bangor, Maine, 1769–2009.* Additional works are underway. Dr. Scee lives in the Bangor area.

Visit us at
www.historypress.net